KENYA

Claude Hervé-Bazin

JPMGUIDES

Contents

🟡	**This Way Kenya**	3
🟠	**Flashback**	7
🔴	**On the Scene**	11
	Nairobi	11
	The Great National Parks	17
	The Rift Valley	24
	The West	30
	The Highlands	33
	The North	36
	The Coast	40
🟢	**Cultural Notes**	52
🟤	**Dining Out**	54
🔴	**Shopping**	56
🟢	**Sports**	58
🔵	**The Hard Facts**	60
🟫	**Tanzania**	65
🟣	**On Safari**	93
	Wildlife Checklist	125
	Index	127

Maps

Nairobi	12
Mombasa	42
Zanzibar (city)	75
Zanzibar (island)	77
Kenya	fold-out
Tanzania	fold-out

This Way Kenya

Animal Kingdom

Deep in the heart of African safari country, Kenya is everything you ever imagined the Dark Continent to be. Its very name conjures up pictures of vast herds of elephant lumbering over the rolling, grassy plains, beneath the shadow of snow-capped Mount Kilimanjaro.

For many, Kenya is synonymous with big game—and for good reason. With a land area almost two and a half times that of the United Kingdom (582,600 sq km or 225,000 sq miles), the country has more than fifty national parks and game reserves, covering 8 per cent of its territory—roughly a third of the size of England! Many of its parks are known worldwide: Masai Mara, with its countless, varied fauna; Amboseli, at the foot of Kilimanjaro; Tsavo, for its huge numbers of elephant; Lake Nakuru, for its clouds of pink flamingos. The premier destination in Africa, Kenya offers the possibility of observing and capturing (on film) virtually all the large animal species of the continent. The Big Five—namely buffalo, elephant, leopard, lion and rhinoceros—are more numerous here than anywhere else.

And they are not alone. You are also likely to come across cheetah, troops of baboons and packs of hyenas, yawning hippopotami and graceful giraffes, wart hogs bounding away with their stiff bristly tails in the air, zebras and thousands of antelopes, great and small. If you're really lucky, you may get the chance to watch the big cats hunting prey, or see the momentous annual migration of the wildebeest. In summer, a vast herd of over a million animals tramples over the savannah of the Masai Mara in search of new grass. As the first animals cross the river, impelled by the moving hordes coming up behind, the crocodiles lie in wait, ready for a tasty meal after a long fast.

Lie of the Land

Straddling the equator, and a cornerstone between the shores of the Indian Ocean and Lake Victoria, Kenya has two distinct sides to its character, shaped by the circumstances of its history and geography. On the one hand, the area along the coast constantly absorbed and adapted to foreign influence, ever since Arab navigators landed there in the 8th and 9th centuries. But the mysterious interior remained in the hands of local tribes right up to the 19th century, undisturbed apart from the murderous incursions of slave traders. It is here, on the high plains and along the Rift Valley, that most of the national parks and reserves are found today. It's virtually impossible to define a natural unity; Kenya is made up of a veritable kaleidoscope of fascinating landscapes and personalities.

In the west, the great fault of the Rift Valley slashes through Kenya from north to south. One of the world's most famous geological formations, it stretches all the way from the Middle East to southern Africa. According to a number of specialists, it will one day become a new ocean. Along it is a string of eight lakes, some of them freshwater, others alkaline—the happy hunting grounds of countless species of bird, including the emblematic pink flamingo that gather here by the million every winter. Far to the north, anthropologists have discovered fragments of bone dating back millions of years on the banks of Lake Turkana, permitting them to identify the Rift Valley as the cradle of humanity.

Further west again, the old White Highlands of colonial times still remain the centre of Kenyan agriculture—tea, coffee and flowers being the main crops. The shores of Lake Victoria are densely inhabited by a farming population. The region shelters the last vestiges of the ancient humid tropical forest that once covered the whole centre of black Africa.

To the north, beyond Mount Kenya and the fertile Kikuyu lands where tea and coffee are cultivated, stretch the limitless wastes of the desert. More than a third of the country disappears into the bounds of Somalia and Ethiopia, an inhospitable, barren territory where only a few nomadic tribes roam. Here and there, an oasis emerges from the wilderness: the Samburu reserve on the banks of the Ewaso Nyiro river, which fizzles out before it can reach the ocean; the rocky peak and forest of Marsabit, further to the north.

A different world opens up as you approach the shores of the Indian Ocean. The air becomes more humid, the sun seems to shine more intensely. A beach unfurls more than 500 km (300 miles) from north to south along the coast, a paradise for divers and perfect for those who just want to relax beneath the coconut palms.

The pastoral Samburu live in the north of Kenya, in a region of semi-desert.

The Towns

Clustered on an island just off the coast, Mombasa is Kenya's second-largest city, a former trade centre with Arabia, India and the Far East. Despite its being an industrial port, Mombasa has a decidedly tropical atmosphere, and life goes on at an easy-going pace. Wandering through the intricate tangle of little streets of the old town, you'll soon sense a trace of nostalgia that stirs memories of a past still lingering in the present. Dotted here and there along the coast are dozens of ancient cities built by Arab conquerors. While some of the ruins are wonderfully preserved, others have been so dilapidated by the passage of time that they are hardly recognizable.

Light-years away in the centre of the country, Nairobi is a modern and cosmopolitan city, if a little untidy, like any other big African capital. Most of the international organizations that work in East Africa have chosen Nairobi as their headquarters, taking advantage of the political stability of the country as well as the cooler climate of the plains. Gateway to the principal wildlife reserves, Nairobi is the focus of all the nation's activities, developing at an alarming pace. Its hotels are up to top international standards, and many of them are built in the colonial style.

The Peoples

Apart from its obvious natural attractions, Kenya is one of the African countries with the greatest cultural diversity. The 25 million-strong population is made up of no fewer than 48 different ethnic groups.

In the interior, the minority cultures have jealously maintained their ancient traditions. Among the better known are the pastoral Masai, who live mainly in the south an eastern lowlands. Their taste for the nomadic way of life and their particular fondness for personal adornment is shared by several other tribes, for example the Samburu, who live further north and who, like the Rendille, breed camels. The Turkana, and their neighbours the Pokots, are a little more timid. The Kikuyu, in the central highlands, form the largest group and until recent times have traditionally been dominant in commerce and politics.

The coastal region's history goes back some ten centuries. This area was long the crossroads of Africa and Arabia, colonized by Omani sultans. Visible signs of their occupation have endured, along with a particular cultural heritage. Like its language, Swahili, the civilization is a cocktail of religions, beliefs and customs, a marriage between the Middle East and the Dark Continent.

Flashback

The Dawn of Humanity

In the last part of the 20th century, one discovery after another in the Rift Valley has confirmed that Kenya is at the heart of the birthplace of humanity. Most of the fossils discovered were buried around the shores of Lake Turkana. Anthropologists believe that it was in this region that the evolution of man went in a different direction from that of the ape. As the climate changed and the land gradually turned into desert, he began to stand upright and learned to run, for speed was a great advantage in crossing the wide unsheltered spaces.

Unearthed at the beginning of the 1970s, the 300 fragments of Cranium 1470—its inventory number at the Nairobi Museum—were the first to breach the million-year barrier. With an estimated age of 2.5 million years, it was the earliest *Homo habilis* to be found. Then came Lucy, the remains of an *Australopithecus afarensis* some 3.2 millions of years old, brought to light in Ethiopia in 1974. Since then, thanks to the discoveries of Kenyan anthropologists Louis, Mary and Richard Leakey, our knowledge of early man goes even further back in time. In August 1995, bone fragments estimated at 3.9 to 4.2 million years old were dug up. A new branch was added to mankind's family tree, that of *Australopithecus anamensis*.

First Contacts

Recorded history in East Africa began with the dawn of the Christian era. In his *Periplus of the Erythraean Sea*, a Greek merchant living in Egypt relates his experiences and gives an eye-witness account of the existing trading network between the Persian Gulf, India and East Africa. In the 2nd century, the Greek geographer and astronomer Ptolemy described the colonies on the East African coast and speculated on the whereabouts of the source of the Nile. His *Geography* remained the accepted authority until the great European explorations of the 15th and 16th centuries.

Arabs and Persians

During the 8th and 9th centuries, Arabs and Persian Muslims started appearing more and more around the eastern seaboard of Africa. Trading posts were established on the islands of the Lamu archipelago. Glassware, textiles, wheat and wine were exchanged for ivory, rhinoceros horn and slaves.

Little by little, Arabs colonized the entire coast. They intermingled with the African population, and from this union the Swahili culture was born, a mixture of Arab civilization and African beliefs. The towns of Mombasa and Malindi, Pate and Gedi developed rapidly, but they often clashed in fratricidal attempts to dominate trading.

The Portuguese

In 1498, the Portuguese navigator Vasco da Gama sailed round the Cape of Good Hope and reached the east coast of Africa. Welcomed by the Sultan of Malindi (who was at war with his neighbour in Mombasa at the time), da Gama concluded a military and trading alliance with him. After several attacks, Mombasa finally fell into the hands of Francisco de Almeida and his men in 1505. The town was pillaged, and was to suffer the same fate on three further occasions before the Portuguese could settle permanently in what became their regional capital. Strategically placed on the route to India, Mombasa was the centre of trade on the Indian Ocean. To protect their prize, the Portuguese built Fort Jesus in 1593 and placed the city under the authority of their ally the Sheikh of Malindi.

The struggle for commercial and religious supremacy—each belligerent claiming to be fighting a holy war—continued throughout the 17th century. The beginning of the century was marked by the overwhelming supremacy of the Portuguese, but gradually the colony was engulfed. In 1698, Fort Jesus fell into the hands of the Omani Arabs after a three-year siege. When the enemy troops embarked on the final assault, only 13 of the original 3,000 inhabitants were still alive. Shortly afterwards, the Portuguese were driven out of the region definitively, and a number of Omani families took over the government of the coastal towns, which became city-states.

1

THE MOST BEAUTIFUL SUNRISE At the hour when the muezzin calls the faithful to prayer and the morning air is still cool, go down to the edge of the Indian Ocean. From the old town of **Mombasa**, in the rosy glow of dawn, watch the dhows bobbing gently on the rhythmic swell of the waves.

The Omanis

The 18th century saw a steady worsening of the wars between the city-states. Internal strife between Omanis and Swahilis resulted in an unprecedented economic decline. Change came with the arrival of Seyyid Said on the throne of Oman at the beginning of the 19th century. In 1822 he sent his armies into the East African colonies to curb the activities of the rebellious tribes. In 1840 he moved his capital to Zanzibar, from where he exercised his authority all along the coast. He introduced the cultivation of cloves and reorganized the slave-trade. European and American merchants settled in the area and commerce flourished anew.

The British

As the century progressed, European interest in the region intensified. British and German explorers attempted to discover the elusive source of the Nile. Speke arrived at Lake Victoria in 1858; in 1883 Thomson came through Masai territory. African lands were distributed among the great nations by the terms of the Treaty of Berlin in 1885; Great Britain was given sovereignty over the area covered now by Kenya and Uganda, as well as Zanzibar. This territory became the East Africa Protectorate in 1895 thanks to a pact extorted from the Masai.

Birth of a Town

The following year, the site of the future Nairobi was chosen as base camp for the construction of a railway to link Mombasa with Lake Victoria—then known as "the Lunatic Line". Thirty-two thousand Indian labourers (ancestors of Kenya's currently large Indian population) forged ahead with the track. Nairobi began to take shape: around the core of permanent buildings, a bazaar stretched in all directions. In 1907, the colonial administration moved to the town, where the climate was healthier than at the coast, 500 km (300 miles) away. In 1910, 600 of the 14,000 inhabitants were Europeans.

Colonization forced the Masai to give up their best lands and withdraw to a reserve; the Kikuyu were driven from the fertile high plateaux. Under the influence of Lord Delamere, English gentlemen-farmers launched into mixed agriculture and began to produce coffee. Interrupted by World War I, displacement of the tribes resumed after the end of the conflict. In June 1920, the East Africa Protectorate became the Crown Colony of Kenya.

Towards Independence

During the period between the two world wars, the seeds of discontent were sown by the Kikuyu, the principal victims of expropriation. With Harry Thuku as its leader, the Young Kikuyu Association was created in 1921 and soon became the mouthpiece for the anti-British movement. Among its objectives were the restitution of territory, reduction of taxes, and withdrawal of the system of restricted movement. However, the colonial governors were watching: many of the African leaders were imprisoned and protest stifled.

During World War II, some 100,000 Kenyans were conscripted into the British Army. Kenyan forces took part in the defeat of the Italians in Ethiopia in 1941 and later fought in the Burma campaign against the Japanese, but the lack of recognition after their return renewed controversy. Jomo Kenyatta became head of the nationalist movement in 1947, and the 1952 uprising of Mau-Mau (originally a Kikuyu secret society) threw the country into chaos. All the African leaders were imprisoned. Repression was severe; 13,000 Africans were killed while only around a hundred settlers lost their lives. Nevertheless the tide could not be reversed.

The Republic

With the 1960s came the expansion of African nationalism. Independence was declared in the Sudan in 1956 and in the Gold Coast (Ghana) the following year, accelerating the course of events. The Lancaster House Conference in London in 1960 gave Africans the majority in both the Legislature and the Council of Ministers. In 1961 the KANU party was formed, and a short time later Kenyatta was released. Independence was proclaimed in 1963 and Kenya became a republic. President Kenyatta died in 1978 and was succeeded by Daniel Arap Moi. Mwai Kibaki, founder of the Democratic Party, won the 2002 General Elections. New elections are scheduled for December 2007.

THE TWO MOST BEAUTIFUL ARAB CITIES Only ruins remain of the many city-states that flourished in the Middle Ages. While we can only guess at the past of **Gedi**, which disappeared with the 18th century, **Lamu**, further to the north, is more like a living museum. Its labyrinthine streets, lined with houses of coral stone with heavy carved doors, echo with the memories of a thousand years of history.

On the Scene

For the sake of convenience, Kenya can be divided into two parts: the coastal region and the interior. But it's a little more complex than that, for the interior has many facets. The capital Nairobi, the national parks, the Rift Valley, the largely agricultural west, the central highlands and the northern desert each has a unique culture and landscape; each is, indeed, a different world.

NAIROBI
The City, Excursions

The skyscrapers of the nation's capital stand over what was 100 years ago just a remote, uninhabited watering hole in the highlands. Its Masai name means "place of cold waters", and that was good enough for the British to choose it as base camp for their railway from Mombasa to Lake Victoria. Today it is a bustling modern capital at the crossroads of East Africa, with a population of 2.8 million.

More cosmopolitan and international than African, its compact centre of highrises and its spreading suburbs that range from the chic (Westlands and Langata) to the decidedly less chic (Banana Hills), are typical of any great metropolis anywhere in the world. Nairobi—as everywhere else in the country—has a steadily increasing population and all the problems that go with it. Real estate is continually expanding, and new buildings pop out of the ground like mushrooms.

The town's generally pleasant and temperate climate make it an ideal starting point for exploring the game parks of the interior—or fine place to relax after a safari. Lions roar a mere 8 km (5 miles) from the city centre, in Nairobi National Park, while tea plantations cling to the foothills of the high plateaux.

The City
Carefully planned right from the beginning, Nairobi has kept its tidy, purposeful appearance. However, since independence it

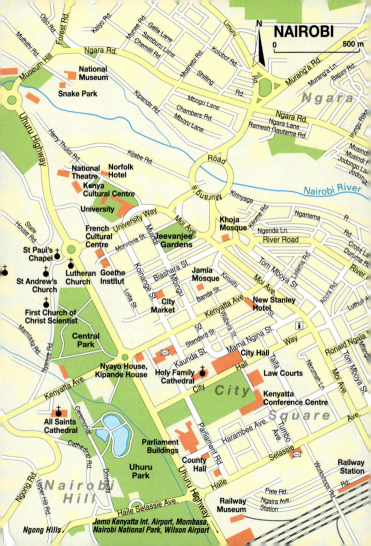

is gradually becoming more and more African in character; from the riotous marketplace to the improvised stalls of small-time hawkers, it's as colourful as a kaleidoscope.

The Centre

Bounded by Uhuru Highway to the west, Haile Selassie Avenue to the south, Moi Avenue to the east and University Way to the north, the town centre is the beating heart of Nairobi. All the shops and trades, offices, restaurants and most of the large hotels are clustered in this area.

The imposing centrepiece and a good place to start your sightseeing is the huge Kenyatta Conference Centre overlooking City Square. Its cylindrical honeycomb effect owes little to its African roots, but the next-door amphitheatre is shaped like a rondavel (African hut) and nicely balances its neighbour. From the 28th floor (entry is free but a tip is expected), the view over Nairobi extends to the west as far as the Ngong Hills, the bastion of the British in Kenya.

The Centre forms a strange contrast to the quintessentially English neoclassical Law Courts, built during colonial times. Across the road are the parliament buildings. If you'd like to see African democracy at work, you can obtain permission to sit in at one of its sessions. Beyond stretch the city's lungs, Central and Uhuru parks (but don't go there after dusk). You can also visit the National Archives, opposite the Hilton on Moi Avenue. There's an interesting ethnographical collection and even an art gallery.

National Museum

Take a taxi to visit the splendid National Museum, a mile from the town centre. Its anthropological and palaeontological departments provide an exhilarating visual account of Africa's prehistory with fossilized remains of prehistoric animals and the fossilized human bones which identified Kenya (specifically the Rift Valley) as the cradle of humanity. Pride of place goes to the renowned Cranium 1470, at the time it was discovered the oldest known *Homo habilis* skull.

There is a large ornithological collection and some awe-inspiringly large present-day animals, stuffed. Other displays include collections of local and tribal crafts, together with an attractive illustration of Swahili culture.

Opposite the museum is the Snake Park, where you can see all manner of snakes, crocodiles and lizards. Once a week (usually on Wednesdays), it is possible to watch the snakes being milked for their venom.

> **LUNATIC LINE**
>
> The Railway Museum on Station Road celebrates the city's beginnings as HQ for the old "Lunatic Line". Glistening relics of the trains are exhibited, along with the coach from which lion-hunter Charles Ryall, a superintendant of the railways, was dragged to his death at Kima in 1900. The poor man sat up in this coach all night in the hope of catching a man-eating lion that had been terrorizing the track gangs, but he fell asleep and it was the beast that caught him.

Tea Time

On your way back to town, stop for a pot of tea at the Norfolk Hotel (on Harry Thuku Road), a relic of colonial days. Built in 1904, it used to be the social centre of British society. It is still very popular today for those who like to drink their tea with a spoonful of nostalgia.

In the same category, but in the centre of town, the New Stanley Hotel is something of an institution. Built a little later than the Norfolk, it has the most fashionable café in Nairobi, the Thorn Tree Café, named after the acacia which was planted in the middle of the terrace at the time of its construction.

Excursions

Conveniently situated almost on the doorstep of the capital, close to the airport, the Nairobi National Park is ideal for making acquaintance with Kenya and good preparation for a safari.

Nairobi National Park

Created in 1945, in a zone of dry savannah interspersed by shady valleys, this was Kenya's first national park. Smaller and more compact than the game sanctuaries further afield, the beautiful, well-kept park contains a satisfying number of Africa's best-known animals—gazelle, zebra, giraffe and buffalo, lion, leopard and cheetah, that may well prove to be more camera-friendly than those in the bush. In fact they are so used to visitors that they keep still and you could almost swear they were posing for pictures.

The park is one of the best places in Kenya to observe rhinos, which have been gathered here in considerable numbers as they are easier to protect closer to the city. In the southeast of the reserve, you can walk through an acacia forest and try to spot hippopotamus and crocodile sunning themselves on the banks of the River Athi. During the migratory season—September in particular—herds of wildebeest (the preferred term nowadays for what is more sympathetically known as

EXCURSIONS

Colourful arcades make a bright splash along River Road.

gnu) reach the park in search of grass. The only animal you won't see is the elephant.

The Animal Orphanage close to the entrance is a home for young abandoned animals unable to cope for themselves in the wild, specially effective in taking care of elephants.

Bomas of Kenya

Beyond the National Park in the direction of Langata, the Bomas of Kenya is a governmental cultural centre, a collection of traditional houses that showcase the different cultures of the country. You can watch performances of the songs and dances of 16 tribes. The most interesting are by the Samburu, the Wakamba and the Mjikenda. There are also demonstrations of tribal crafts and a shop. The shows take place at 2.30 p.m. during the week and at 3.30 p.m. on weekends.

Giraffe Centre

At Langata, this is a sort of open-air museum where you will learn everything you ever wanted to know about the giraffe. You can also feed the Rothschild giraffes wandering freely in the grounds of Giraffe Manor (an elegant private property reminiscent of the colonial past). From a circular platform 3 m (10 ft) above ground, you offer buckets of cereals to the giant creatures—giving you the rare chance of a close-up view of a tongue 45 cm (18 in) long.

Karen Blixen Museum

In the Karen quarter adjoining Langata, the Karen Blixen Museum has been set up in the farm of the Danish writer (pen name Isak Dinesen) made famous by the film *Out of Africa*. Her house is the archetype colonial residence of the early 20th century. Apart from numerous animal skins on the floors and walls, you can see the baroness's bathtub, uncomfortable to say the least.

Close by, visit the Karen Racecourse, a favourite weekend meeting-place for the descendants of the white settlers who came before independence.

Limuru

For more nostalgia, visit the heights of Limuru further west, in the direction of the Rift Valley. Plantations of tea and coffee in carefully aligned rows like corduroy cover the valleys in an impressive patchwork of colours. Several operators arrange visits to Kiambethu Tea Estate at Tigoni, belonging to one of the first families to plant tea here. You will see all the stages of production, and hear the family history.

Hidden in the hills, the Kentmere Club is the quintessential white colonists' club, a bit of England transported to the heart of Africa.

> **BEWARE OF THE GIRAFFE**
>
> An unexpected consequence of the countless numbers of animals in Kenya: in the immediate post-war years when aircraft were still small and fragile, pilots had to make several passes over the runway beside the nature reserve, to clear the strip of antelope and giraffe before they could land.

> **THE THREE MOST BEAUTIFUL BIG CATS** The main ambition of most visitors is to have a sighting of the **lion** and his discreet cousin the **leopard**, both belonging to the *Panthera* family. The exclusive member of the *Acinonyx* family, the **cheetah**, can beat them both in a race: his 70 mph has made him so famous that he almost puts the others in the shade.

THE GREAT NATIONAL PARKS
Masai Mara, Amboseli, Tsavo

Local history has always been influenced by the presence of big game. When the Arab traders first came to this area, it was in quest of ivory. Later, in the 19th century, the abundance of wildlife, and in particular the bigger animals, began to attract western trophy-hunters, among their numbers Ernest Hemingway and Theodore Roosevelt. The latter single-handedly shot some 300 animals during a visit in 1910—including 9 lions and 13 rhinoceros. The settlers also hunted, partly for necessity but often for sport.

Concern for Nature
Fortunately, others were worried about the future of the species, and after World War II the first nature reserves were created, thanks to the efforts of various ecological groups.

Today, Kenya is one of the leaders in Africa for nature conservation. There are 51 parks and reserves in all, scattered across the country, varying in size from a few square miles to the size of Israel. Most are in the interior, but there are also several marine reserves.

Apart from the Masai Mara, which is a continuation of the Serengeti park on the other side of the border with Tanzania, the leading destinations are Amboseli, at the foot of Mount Kilimanjaro, and Tsavo, one of the biggest parks in the world.

Safari
A visit to any of these parks is guaranteed to provide unforgettable memories. You will have countless opportunities to observe the wildlife. If you are interested in seeing one species in particular, you can inquire as to their whereabouts, but remember that they never stay in the same place, that the climatic conditions vary and that the availability of

---

PARK OR RESERVE?

In practice, the national parks are administered at a national level whereas the reserves are controlled by local authorities. In a country where the population grows at an alarming rate, this distinction is vital: local governments can choose to modify the frontiers and the size of the reserves. In this way, a few years ago, the Masai Mara lost 10 per cent of its area for the benefit of the local herdsmen and farmers.

THE GREAT NATIONAL PARKS

The summit of Kilimanjaro revealed at the close of day.

water and food are unpredictable. Do not be disappointed if you don't tick off every great beast on the list.

Some seasons are more favourable than others. The dry season from January until March is usually considered the best, as this is the time the animals gather around the last watering-holes. It's also during this period that you'll see the greatest number of birds on the Rift Valley lakes. But every season has something to offer; for example in July and August you can witness the extraordinary migration of the gnu (wildebeest) with as many as a million animals on the move.

From a practical standpoint, your safari (a Swahili word meaning "journey") usually takes one of two forms. The most popular is to travel through the bush in a four-wheel-drive vehicle or a mini-bus with open roof, either of which allows you to get very close to the animals. In general, you leave the lodge early in the morning for a first game drive which lasts until breakfast. Dawn is the best time for observing African wildlife, in particular to watch the big cats (leopard, lion) hunting. A second excursion takes you to lunch time. After a siesta during the heat of the day —when the animals also rest under cover—you set off again for your third game drive which lasts until sunset.

The second option is to choose a lodge overlooking a wateringhole or a saltlick; in which case you don't have to go chasing all over the savannah searching for animals but can simply sit and wait until they come to you. Some camps even have bells in the rooms to let you know that a herd of elephants is arriving, or that there's a leopard on the prowl. And for those requiring something more exotic, there are camel safaris, ox-wagon safaris and balloon safaris to choose from.

Masai Mara

The Mara, as the Kenyans call it, is the most visited and perhaps the most beautiful of all the country's game reserves. Covering an area of 1,510 sq km (almost 600 sq miles), it is part of the traditional Masai lands, and its edges are dotted with *manyats*, the shepherds' villages. It's an integral part of the Serengeti ecosystem, divided in two by the vagaries of human geography. The wildlife is abundant all year round.

Stretching as far as the eye can see, the savannah of the Mara is dotted with clumps of trees, vestiges of the ancient forest which

---

THE MASAI

Despite their small number (about 650,000) the Masai are the best-known of the Kenyan tribes. Nomadic, warfaring herdsmen, of Nilotic origin, they made their mark in history by fiercely opposing British colonization. Today they live in the south of Kenya, close to the Amboseli and Masai Mara parks.

Masai life is centred around the cattle which provide their food (not only the milk, but also blood taken from the jugular vein), their leather supply and their entire wealth. The supreme punishment for a man condemned by the tribe is to have his cattle confiscated. Their existence follows a very structured pattern, marked by a series of ritual ceremonies. Youths are initiated at 14 years or older, when they become moranes. For the ensuing period of nine years, they learn to live away from their families in small groups and to become true warriors. After this apprenticeship, they are consecrated in a ceremony called *Eunoto* as "elders", and only then are they allowed to marry.

long ago covered most of the area. An explosion of the gnu population—from 300,000 during the 1950s to well over a million today—has led to overgrazing and a consequent increase in the size of the open plains. If you visit the park in summer, you will no doubt see the wondrous sight of hundreds of thousands of gnu and zebra on the move, in search of fresh grass, having stripped the Serengeti bare. Later, driven on by the arrival of new herds, the first animals ford the River Mara. This perilous crossing undertaken by hordes of maddened beasts is truly dramatic: many of them drown, others get bogged down in the mud and die. Their great numbers attract predators, so it is one of the best opportunities you'll have to observe the big cats hunting.

The Animal Kingdom

The lion is king of the jungle and rules over the Mara. The reserve is famous for its thousand lions, the males sporting a particularly dark and shimmering mane. Each pride is made up of about 30 animals, idling away the daylight hours and stirring only at dawn and at dusk.

To watch the lions hunting is a rare privilege, but they are not as gifted as you might have imagined. Indeed, statistics show that many predators put on a very mediocre performance. Lions and leopards let 80 per cent of their prey get away, while the hyena has a failure rate of 65 per cent. The champions are the hunting dogs (lycaon), though these animals have become rare and are not easy to spot. The leopard is also elusive, but they do tend to let their tails dangle down from branches, so keep your eyes open. The cheetah, who spends most of the day out on the grassy savannah, is more easily observed.

Elephant are found in the wooded zones. They number about a thousand in the park, living in herds of some twenty members. You may also see one of the Mara's 20 rhinos. There are many giraffe and buffalo and countless antelopes: Thomson's gazelle, Grant's gazelle, impalas, dik-diks and topis. At Hippo Pools on the River Mara, a colony of hippopotamus squelch around in the shallow waters, which they share with crocodile.

For a unique experience (though it's fairly expensive), book a place for the morning flight in one of the park's hot-air balloons, and glide serenely above the immensity of the savannah in an unearthly silence.

The eyes of this Masai lady from Namanga reflect a fearless dignity.

Amboseli

Kenya's second most popular park in terms of numbers of visitors, Amboseli benefits from the most beautiful backdrop of all the parks—the grandiose snow-covered table peak of Kilimanjaro. The extinct volcano itself in fact rises across the Tanzanian border, with only its northern foothills within Kenya's boundaries. "As wide as all the world, great, high and unbelievably white in the sun" wrote Hemingway in his short story *The Snows of Kilimanjaro*. The highest point of the African continent at 5,891 m (19,328 ft), the mountain has a circumference at the base of over 160 km (about 100 miles). It has three peaks, of which the highest, named Uhuru ("liberty"), looms over the Kibo plateau.

The 389 sq km (152 sq miles) of park are largely arid lands of acacia and tall savannah grasses. In such an exposed landscape the animals are easy to observe. In places, subterranean springs have transformed the plain into marshland. Constantly changing, the springs have a determining influence on life in the park. In recent times infiltrated by salt water, they are modifying the ecosystem, causing the loss of certain plant species. The continual changes can, however, have a beneficial effect: the general rise of the water table now attracts increasing numbers of pink flamingos and pelicans. To the west, the park is bordered by Lake Amboseli, dry for most of the year.

Elephant Country

Elephant is the emblem of Amboseli and they are everywhere, about five animals per square mile. It's no doubt a cliché, but a herd of elephant lumbering along beneath the snowy summit of Kilimanjaro is a sight you'll never forget. At the end of the afternoon, make your way to the banks of the River Sinet to watch the elephant family at their daily shower. You will also see giraffe, zebra, and perhaps leopard, cheetah, buffalo and rhinoceros. The antelope family is represented by the kudu with its slender spiral horns, the long-necked gerenuk and the oryx. In the marshy zones there are also hippopotamus, elephant and a multitude of birds. But there's only one pair of lions.

As you travel around the park, do not be surprised to see grazing cattle. Although Amboseli's statute as a national park forbids the Masai to bring their herds to the watering-holes, they ignore the rules. Conflicting interests are an eternal problem in this drought-stricken land. At least you will have the opportunity to see the costumes and spears of the warriors at close hand.

Tsavo

Covering more than 20,000 sq km (7,800 sq miles), Tsavo is the largest national park in Kenya, and one of the largest in the world. It is divided into two parts, Tsavo West, the most visited, and Tsavo East, where the northern boundary is still closed to the public. Crossed by the Nairobi-Mombasa road, the park is easily accessible from either of these two towns.

The western sector is the most interesting and the most varied, presenting diverse and contrasting landscapes. Stretching to infinity, the plains are dotted with volcanic cones, and there's dense savannah, rocky hills, and humid forest along the River Tsavo. More than 60 species of mammal and 500 of bird live within its confines.

Mzima Springs

This will probably be your first stop; it's an oasis whose two natural pools are home to a large hippopotamus colony. You can watch their antics from the top of an observation tower, and perhaps also be lucky enough to spot some crocodile. For a close-up view of the hippos in their natural environment, head for the observation tank ingeniously built into one of the pools. You can watch their fat legs paddling about in the crystal-clear water. Not far away, at Roaring Rocks, an observation tower has been set up and enables you to see far into the interior of the park.

Endangered Species

The rhinoceros population, virtually wiped out by poachers in the 1980s, is gradually multiplying around the Ngulia Rhino Sanctuary. The crash of rhinoceros at Tsavo now numbers almost 200. The elephant population is also increasing; by the end of the 1960s it had reached a maximum of almost 23,000 animals altogether, distributed in large herds. At one time, it was even claimed that seasonal gatherings attained as many as 15,000 animals. Whittled down to only 3,000 individuals in 1985, they have today been saved from extinction, as poaching has been practically eliminated.

You have a better chance of seeing large herds in the east. Make the short climb up the Mudanda Rock—a miniature version of Australia's Ayers Rock—and from the summit you have an unimpeded view of the watering-hole to the east. Buffalo and elephant often gather there. Notice the dark-red mudpack coating the elephants' hides: it protects them from sunburn and insect bites. Further east, the sandbanks and rocks along the Galana River are the haunt of crocodile.

THE RIFT VALLEY
Lake Naivasha, Hell's Gate, Lake Nakuru, Lake Bogoria, Lake Baringo

At the end of the 19th century, the Austrian geologist Eduard Suess put forward the theory that a fault runs through the earth's crust from Syria in southwestern Asia to Mozambique in southeastern Africa, passing through the Dead Sea, the Red Sea, Ethiopia's Afars Depression, Kenya's Lake Turkana and Tanzania as far as Lake Malawi—a total distance of more than 4,830 km (3,000 miles).

In 1893, one of his colleagues, a Scot called John Walter Gregory (known as "Full-pockets" because they were always bulging with stones), discovered a rocky plaque of stratified layers, tilted on its side, at the bottom of the valley near Lake Baringo. The layers matched those of the cliffs bordering the depression, proving that the earth's crust had sunk to form a trough.

In their search for the cause of continental drift, geologists discovered the existence of chains of submarine volcanoes, formed by upward surges of magma from the earth's mantle (where the continental plates are formed). Deep troughs were created all along the axis of these submerged mountains, which became known as oceanic rifts. The Rift Valley and Iceland are the only places on earth where these rifts have emerged from the sea. In eastern Africa it separates into two branches: the eastern and western rifts; the latter rejoins the main fault at Lake Malawi.

A Unique System

Varying in width from a few kilometres to 160 km (100 miles) along its entire length, the Rift reaches a depth of almost 2,700 m (9,000 ft) in places. It is still sinking, dropping a few more millimetres each year. At the same time, its sides are drifting further and further apart, at the rate of several centimetres per year. If the trend continues, it should give rise to a new ocean cutting East Africa off from the rest of the continent in the same way that the Atlantic Ocean was formed. But the process will take some 20 or 30 million years. The Red Sea is the first, northerly indication of the split, while further evidence is provided by the great bodies of water in the western rift (lakes Edward, Tanganyika, Albert, etc.). Along the uplifted edges of the valley, a series of volcanoes, Kilimanjaro, Mount Kenya, Mount Egon, for instance, act as safety valves.

The Lakes

Apart from its geological interest, the Rift Valley is particularly famous for its eight lakes. They appeared some 40 million years ago, when they spread over the basalt floor of the depression. Since then they have greatly reduced in size due to the climatic conditions. In the lakes that have no outlet, the waters have become an alkaline concentration of minerals that would at first seem hostile to all forms of life—these are the soda lakes, Bogorio, Nakuru, Elmenteita, Magadi and Natron. Nevertheless, bacteria and algae have flourished in this environment, providing nourishment for flamingos that flock here in their millions at certain times of the year in an amazing flurry of pink feathers.

Freshwater Baringo and Naivasha also attract an impressive number of birds, in particular many migrating species, while hippopotamus congregate along the shores. Several of the lakes are preserved as national parks, and their immediate surroundings are home to many kinds of mammal, some of them easy to observe, others more timid.

Lake Naivasha

In the heart of a fertile agricultural area, an hour's drive northwest of Nairobi, Lake Naivasha is particularly famous for its rich bird life. More than 400 species have been spotted in this bird-watcher's paradise: pelicans, cormorants, herons, gallinules and long-toed jacanas (more daintily known as lily trotters) are readily observed. The best way to see them is to hire a boat for Crescent Island, a bird sanctuary a short distance from the eastern shore. In spring you can walk around the island to see the nesting colonies. If you are there during a different season, you will sight many other animals. Don't get too close to the defassa waterbuck, a large brown antelope with lyre-shaped horns: it can become aggressive if cornered.

Elsamere

On the southwest bank of Lake Naivasha, Elsamere is the former home of Austrian-born Joy Adamson, who gained celebrity thanks to her book *Born Free*, about the lioness Elsa. She and her husband George, a British game warden, devoted their lives to reintroducing into their native habitat cats that had been held captive in European and American zoos and circuses. After their separation, Joy continued her work at Elsamere, where she did much of her writing, and George moved to Kora National Reserve in the east of the country. At a time when poaching was at its peak in East Africa, Joy was mur-

Birds of a pink feather flocking together on Lake Nakuru.

dered by tribesmen in the Shaba Reserve in 1980. Nine years later, her husband was killed by Somali poachers in Kora. Elsamere is now a conservation centre, open to the public every afternoon. A visit here includes a viewing of the film *The Joy Adamson Story,* relating her fight to protect the environment. Afternoon tea is included in the entrance fee, and it is possible to spend the night there.

Hell's Gate

Immediately south of Lake Naivasha, the small Hell's Gate is one of the rare national parks where you are allowed to get out of your car and walk around, mainly because there are no dangerous animals. The landscape is dominated by an escarpment of volcanic rock and by Hell's Gate Gorge—a one-time outflow of Lake Naivasha—both spectacular and a haven for numerous animals. The park is one of the rare nesting sites of the crested vulture.

Lake Nakuru

For bird-lovers (and everyone else), Lake Nakuru offers the most extraordinary winged wonderland you could ever imagine. The lake has the largest flamingo colony in the world. Under particularly suitable conditions, up to 2 million of these birds have been counted, massed in groups of several thousand on the shallow waters. It's hard to find adequate words to describe this incredible sight. Of all the African birds, it's the flamingos that have the richest colouring, "pink and red like a flying twig of an oleander bush", wrote Karen Blixen in *Out of Africa*.

Nakuru's water, like that of other lakes in the Rift Valley, is a concentration of fluid that has washed through volcanic ash; consequently its sodium content is high. The flamingos feed on algae and shrimps which have adapted themselves to these particular ecological conditions; their beak is equipped with a pump and filter system so they can ingurgitate the alkaline soup without any danger. The arrival of the birds and their departure for other lakes is governed by climatic conditions which modify the salinity. During the dry season, the best times to observe them in great numbers are morning and evening.

Clouds of Pink

For a unique view, climb Baboon Cliffs on the west bank of the lake. Down below, the throngs of birds look like a huge Impressionist canvas of flickering pink dots on a blue background.

The largest flocks of flamingos generally gather at Hippo Pools to the north and at Pelican Point to the southwest. Leave your car and walk towards them—with caution, as the ground is unsteady. As you approach, you'll hear the ever-increasing sound of grunting and the beating of wings. Get too close, and there's sudden panic: the water churns and the air fills with salmon-pink feathers as squadrons of birds take to the skies in a turmoil of colour.

Towards the middle of the lake, white pelicans skim the deeper waters in orderly groups. Elsewhere, cormorants, grebes, ibis, storks (in winter), marabous, herons and even fish-eagles can be seen.

This national park has been enlarged since its inauguration in 1961 and now covers some 200 sq km (75 sq miles). It harbours the largest concentration of rhinoceros in Kenya outside the Nairobi Park, brought here for their protection. They can be seen in the southern part of the park. As there are only 500 rhinos in the whole country, the experience is far from commonplace. You'll also encounter the Rothschild giraffe, one of Africa's rarest animals and distinguishable from their more ordinary cousins by a second pair of horns and fetching knee-length white socks. Buffalo

> **KENYAN WINES**
>
> South Africa is not the only country in the continent to produce decent wines. Zimbabwe, Ethiopia and Kenya all have vineyards producing their own vintages. While South African wines now enjoy international renown, the handful of Kenyan whites produced in the Lake Naivasha region are unheard of beyond the country's borders. If you are curious, let yourself be tempted. Some of them might actually be a pleasant surprise.

and defassa waterbuck are numerous, as are the wart hogs which snuffle around in gangs. And, if you are lucky, you may see one of the park's leopards.

Lake Bogoria

The northernmost alkaline lake is also one of the most beautiful, nestling at the foot of the rocky heights of the eastern escarpment of the Rift Valley. The Aberdare Range forms a backdrop against the sky.

On the west shore of the lake, steam rising from hot springs and small geysers drape the scarlet multitudes of flamingos in a misty shawl. As at Lake Nakuru, there is no outlet for the water, and its high mineral content makes it a paradise for waders. It teems with blue-green algae, their favourite food. At times, dwarf flamingos literally carpet the edges of the lake. The colonies are regularly devastated by fish-eagles who are obliged to turn to other birds as sustenance in the absence of fish. You may also see pelicans, cormorants, herons and kingfishers.

An area around the lake has been designated as a reserve for the protection of animals, mainly the greater kudu which is rarely seen elsewhere. This magnificent antelope, light grey with vertical white strips and long, spiral horns comes down to the lake in the evening to drink. There are about a thousand here, though the animal was almost wiped out by rinderpest in the 19th century. Other animals here include leopard, cheetah, jackal and hyena.

Lake Baringo

At the confines of Samburu and Pokot country, on the edge of the vast tracts of semi-desert stretching to the north, freshwater Lake Baringo, in stark contrast to its austere environment, is the premier ornithological destination in Kenya. Birdwatching is a tradition here. Twitchers could not hope for a happier hunting ground: more than 450 different species have been recorded. A

LAKE BARINGO

A flash of chestnut feathers as a Goliath heron flies over Baringo Lake.

few years ago, the full-time ornithologist employed by the Lake Baringo Club established a world record by observing more than 300 species within 24 hours. There are bird-watching walks every morning (7 a.m.) and evening (5 p.m.) and the expert is always ready to answer your questions.

Apart from the pink flamingos that cluster around the landing stage, white pelicans, cormorants, herons, egrets, spoonbills, gallinules and kingfishers are frequently to be seen. The Eurasian winter brings flocks of duck and migrating waders that fly in by the thousand. You can take boat trips and buy fish, and the boatman will whistle for the fish eagles that swoop down to snatch it up.

Other inhabitants of the lake include hippopotamus, relatively numerous and not at all bashful. They stay in the water until nightfall when they browse the grassy banks. They congregate especially around Kampi-ya-Samaki, the chief village of the west bank. Baringo also has a large crocodile population, but this does not seem to deter the lakeside village children from swimming. Apparently the reptiles are not keen on humans. If you believe that, have a go at water-skiing.

THE WEST
Lake Victoria, Kericho, Saiwa Swamp, Mount Elgon

Away from the beaten tourist track, the part of Kenya west of the Rift Valley offers a different aspect of the country. The landscape of undulating hills is covered with round huts, crops and tea plantations; this region is the most densely populated in Kenya. As you approach Lake Victoria, you start to feel the equatorial atmosphere. The country's only tropical rainforest is not far away. Further north, two parks are worth visiting: that of Saiwa Swamp, refuge of the sitatunga antelope, and Mount Elgon, where the elephants have some very strange habits.

Lake Victoria

The biggest lake in Africa with a surface area of more than 68,000 sq km (26,000 sq miles) is shared by Kenya, Uganda and Tanzania. It does not belong to the string of Rift Valley lakes. The Nile, which rises in the mountains of Burundi, flows through it, and it seems more like an immense inland sea than a lake.

Kisumu

The Kenyan shore of the lake is dominated by Kisumu, the third largest city in Kenya. Its climate is frankly equatorial. If you are passing through, take the opportunity to visit the very lively market and the small museum, on Nairobi Road going east. The museum has an interesting section devoted to the traditional habitat of the Luo people, one of the largest tribes of Kenya and who live in this area.

Kakamega Forest

About 50 km (30 miles) north of Kisumu, the Kakamega Reserve contains the last vestige in East Africa of the ancient tropical rainforest which originally stretched all the way to the Atlantic Ocean. The butterfly population is particularly rich; the largest, *Papilio lormieri*, has a wingspan of 13 cm (5 in). Several species of monkey chatter in the foliage, which they share with a large number of birds, among them the rare touraco.

Kericho

At an altitude of 1,700 m (5,500 ft), Kericho enjoys cool evenings. The climate suits the tea plants perfectly: they don't much like the heat and thrive best when the late afternoon brings a touch of frost.

At the very heart of the plantations, Kericho has a wonderful airy atmosphere, perhaps because the whole town is camouflaged

KERICHO • SAIWA SWAMP

A long way to go before it reaches the pot: tea plantations at Kericho.

by a cloak of bright green tea bushes. From one valley to the next, hordes of tea-pickers work their way across the vast, verdant patchwork, plucking the tender young shoots of tea. The whole process of tea production, from sorting to drying and packing, takes place here.

Tea Hotel
At the western exit of Kericho, stay at the Tea Hotel and wallow in nostalgia. Formerly the headquarters of the Brooke Bond Company, it overlooks the earliest plantations and its English gardens are reminiscent of bygone days.

Saiwa Swamp
North of Kitale, near the road leading to Lodwar, the Saiwa Swamp National Park is the smallest in Kenya—2 sq km (less than a square mile) in area. It is unique in that it can only be visited on foot: paths follow the edges of the swamp, and in places raised walkways cross over it. It is also the only place where you can see the sitatunga, the swamp antelope; observation platforms, some of them rather rickety, are perched in the trees.

This shy, delicate antelope with a striped coat has extremely elongated hooves which allow it to move around on the marshy ground without sinking. Perfectly adapted to its environment, it grazes happily on reeds and papyrus while remaining half submerged, and will often disappear entirely below the surface when alarmed.

Mount Elgon

Straddling the Ugandan frontier, Mount Elgon is one of the principal volcanoes created during the formation of the Rift Valley. It has long been dormant, and the only remaining signs of volcanic activity are the few hot springs at the bottom of the caldera. Cliffs, caves and waterfalls and the all-pervading humidity somehow confer on the park the eerie atmosphere of a lost world. The feeling is even more unearthly if you leave the jungle at the end of the track (four-wheel-drive only) and enter the amazing bamboo forest on the upper slopes. Higher still, you come to a region of alpine moorland where humidity and cool temperatures have combined to produce giant vegetation. Groundsel, only a few inches high in Europe, here reaches several feet, and lobelias are more like trees.

Elephant Caves

Despite these wonders, the principal reason for visiting Mount Elgon is to see the caves, and two in particular—Makingeny and Kitum. Try to get there at dawn and you will have every chance of seeing a herd of elephants greedily scraping the salt and minerals from the walls with their tusks. At Kitum, they come virtually every day. The animals go deep into the caves and seem to be able to find their way in total darkness, a skill handed down through the generations. If you, however, are thinking of exploring the caves, remember to take a torch.

THE FOUR BEST-DRESSED TRIBES In the north, several tribes share the desolate territory of the Rift Valley and Lake Turkana. The **Turkana** are fond of striking hairstyles, and sometimes wear lip plugs. The **Pokot** bedeck their arms with heavy copper bracelets, and incorporate plants into their costumes. The **Samburu** have the most beautiful accessories of all: beaded headbands, necklaces and bracelets sometimes weighing several pounds. The **Rendille** adopt the eclectic approach and try a bit of everything.

THE HIGHLANDS
Aberdare Range, Mount Kenya

The rich uplands dominated by the Aberdare Range (named in 1884 after Lord Aberdare, president of the National Geographic Society) and Mount Kenya are the traditional home of the Kikuyu people, who themselves call the range Nyandarua, "drying hide". The land is fertile and intensively cultivated, except for the two national parks centred around the mountain ranges. In spite of agricultural reform, a number of white farmers still run huge estates, mainly producing coffee and tea.

Aberdare Range

Little more than 10 per cent of the Kenyan territory is arable land, and so the Aberdares seem like a blessing for the cultivators. But slowly and surely, the terraced plots are climbing ever higher, encroaching on the last dense forests and causing increasing erosion. Fortunately, a national park preserves the last stretches of virgin forest in central Kenya, a peaceful tract covering 800 sq km (300 sq miles).

Aberdare National Park

The park boundary follows the edge of the Kinangop Plateau—at an altitude of more than 3,000 m (10,000 ft)—and includes a forested area to the east where the two main lodges are situated. Princess Elizabeth was staying at Treetops, the older of the two, when she learnt of her accession to the throne in 1952. Built overlooking waterholes which are illuminated at night, the rooms have bells to let you know when animals come for a drink.

Many species roam the Aberdares: elephant, buffalo and wild boar, rhinoceros and the extremely rare black panther. The bamboo forests are home to a little-seen antelope, the bongo. With spiralling, yellow-tipped horns, the bongo is stocky and distinctively striped. It lives only in dense forest. Therein lies the main problem of the Aberdares—it is often difficult to detect the animals among the foliage. Another disadvantage is that it rains almost all the time, and the paths soon turn into quagmires. To look on the bright side, the rain feeds the many waterfalls, the most beautiful of which is Gura Falls in the south of the park, plunging 300 m (1,000 ft) down into the blanket of vegetation. At higher altitudes, the rain-soaked heathland takes on a spectral, sodden appearance. Above 3,000 m (10,000 ft), the plants grow to gigantic proportions.

Nyahururu

At almost 2,400 m (7,800 ft), Nyahururu is one of the highest towns in Kenya. Perched on a fertile plateau, it is particularly renowned for its waterfalls. On the edge of the town, the Ewaso Narok river cascades over a rocky 70-m (230-ft) cliff, falling into a ravine where its waters are dispersed in a fine mist that sprays over the whole area. From the old Thomson's Falls Lodge, where every room has a fireplace and the atmosphere is quaintly British, the view is simply stunning.

Mount Kenya

Its summit always cloaked in snow, this ancient volcano dominates the entire highland region. At 5,199 m (17,057 ft), it is the second highest mountain in Africa, but geologists estimate that it has been eroded down from an original 6,000 m (19,600 ft). It is scored by glacial valleys, with 11 glaciers and several small lakes. The Kikuyu regarded the mountain as a god, and still today they build their huts so that the doorway opens onto it.

Trekking Routes

Mount Kenya is a foremost destination for trekkers, and there are several routes to the summit. Naro Moru, to the west, is the most popular but the least scenic. The northwest route, Sirimon, is the longest, while Chogoria, to the east, is indisputably the most beautiful. There are other paths, but they are more difficult to follow.

Leaving behind the agricultural land, you walk through the tropical forest, where numerous orchids and other epiphytic plants flourish. The vegetation becomes more sparse, though on certain slopes you have to cross great stands of bamboo reaching up to 15 m (50 ft) in height. After another wooded zone, less leafy than the first, the view opens out onto the wide upper moorland, carpeted with giant heathers, groundsel and lobelia. Higher than 4,500 m (14,500 ft) there's nothing but snow. The easiest climb is to the top of Point Lenana (4,985 m or 16,355 ft), also known as Tourist Peak. Batian and Nelion peaks, respectively 5,199 m (17,057 ft) and 5,188 m (17,022 ft), are for experienced climbers only.

If you are planning an expedition on the mountain, take care—the risks of altitude sickness and hypothermia are very real. At night, the temperature can go down to –10 °C (14°F). You are strongly advised to use the services of a guide.

Mount Kenya reigns like a god over the realm of the Kikuyu.

THE NORTH
Samburu, Matthews Range, Lake Turkana, Marsabit

Discovering the north, Kenya's adventure country, is more like an expedition than tourism. The arid wastes of semi-desert, relieved only by an occasional clump of acacia and the channels of dry river beds, seem to stretch to infinity. The volcanic heritage is apparent everywhere, from the perfect cones rising up from the desert to the rocky lava flows snaking across the landscape. All year long the land sizzles at temperatures reaching up to 50°C (122°F). Here and there an oasis, and a few splashes of high-altitude forest, interrupt the grandiose monotony.

Among the animals to be seen are two species native to the area: the reticulated giraffe whose beautiful coat is patterned like tortoiseshell, outlined in white; and Grevy's zebra, with white belly and narrow, closely-spaced stripes.

In the far north, the ultimate goal of all travellers is Lake Turkana, John Hillaby's *Jade Sea*. The north remains the stronghold of several tribes that stick jealously to their traditions: the Samburu herdsmen, close cousins of the Masai, and the redoubtable Turkana warriors. Each has been allocated a primary zone by the government, but as a result, tribal conflicts have worsened. It is not easy to prevent a tribe from taking what it wants, as every group believes that it has a divine right to all the land and all the cattle in it. Sporadic outbreaks of violence among some of the ethnic groups make the region unsafe, particularly around Lake Marsabit. If you are contemplating a trip to the north, make enquiries about the current situation. The western shores of Lake Turkana are generally clear, but the northeastern sector has been a no-man's-land since armed factions from neighbouring Somalia took over the area.

Samburu

The wild plains of Samburu contain three exceptionally beautiful reserves, Samburu itself, the adjoining Buffalo Springs and Shaba, east of the Isiolo-Marsabit road. Because they are close together and share the same characteristics, they are all described in this section.

Samburu owes its wild beauty to the Ewaso Nyiro, which means "Brown River" in Maa, the common language of the Masai and Samburu peoples. Much further to the east, the river flows into a torrid swamp and peters out before ever reaching the sea. But here its banks are covered with acacias, figs and (in the lower reaches at Shaba) doum palms. Shortly after the rains, the flamboyant colours of the sausage tree *(Kigelia africana)*, the *Delonix elata* (a relation of the flame tree) and a host of wild flowers set the landscape afire.

At Samburu and Buffalo Springs, the vegetation is dense enough to shelter waterbuck, impala and buffalo. Crocodiles soak up the sun on the sandbanks. You can observe them easily from Buffalo Springs Lodge or Samburu Lodge. More discreet, oryx, gazelle, Grevy's zebra, reticulated giraffe, cheetah, lions and leopard keep to the cover provided by the bush, while elephant endlessly patrol the valleys, in herds of a few dozen. You'll probably see the gerenuk, with a long neck like a giraffe, stretching up on the hind legs to nibble the acacia leaves and buds. The gerenuk never drinks; his food supplies all the water his body requires.

Matthews Range

Off the principal tourist routes, some 100 km (60 miles) northwest of Samburu, the Matthews Range remains relatively untouched—though there is a comfortable lodge. These mountains are not classified as a park or a reserve, yet the wildlife is plentiful, particularly elephant, but also buffalo, lion and leopard. There will be no lack of Samburu *moran* volunteering their services as guides—you are in the heart of their territory. Do not hesitate to

THE TURKANA

Numbering almost 250,000, the Turkana live in the northwest of Kenya, mostly between Lake Turkana and Uganda. Of all the Kenyan tribes, they are without doubt the least affected by 20th-century intrusions. Nomadic herdsmen of Nilotic origin, they have become perfectly adapted to their hostile environment.

Warriors by tradition, they cultivate their fighting skills and occasionally put them to use against the neighbouring Rendille and Pokot tribes. The tattoos on the men's shoulders have the same significance as the notches in a gunfighter's belt: marks on the right shoulder record male victims, on the left, females. Witchcraft plays an important part in their society. The Turkana are also known for their bizarre hairstyles—a clump of hair on the crown of the head for the women and decorations of dried mud, tinted blue and stuck with ostrich feathers for the men.

Comfort in the shade at Buffalo Springs Lodge.

accept: their knowledge of the fauna and topography will be more than useful in this densely wooded country.

Lake Turkana

In 1887, Count Samuel Teleki von Szek, a Hungarian aristocrat exiled for having become a little too familiar with a certain Princess Stephanie, explored the unknown tracts of East Africa. He followed the Rift Valley, still uncharted territory at the time, and after 13 months of wandering came to an immense, mirror-like lake. In a fit of generosity, he named it Lake Rudolf in honour of the Habsburg Archduke.

As you approach from the south, an overlook along the track affords a startling view of a lunar landscape that spreads all around, an arid, desolate picture streaked with knotty black veins of solidified lava discharged from gutted volcanoes. By the shore, a few Turkana huts show the small scale of the human population, while in the background shimmers the majestic lake.

Like all the stretches of water in the Rift Valley, Turkana used to occupy a much larger area. Elephants still roamed in the region in the 19th century. Today, however, only Sibiloi National Park, to the northeast, has a small

> **RACING CAMELS**
>
> A great camel race, the International Camel Derby, is held at Maralal every October. As there are three categories (amateur, professional and semi-professional), everyone can join in the fun. Even if you haven't a camel you can always hire one on the spot. Competitors come from the four corners of the earth, but the professional race is invariably won hands down by local jockeys.

animal population, although it was created principally to protect the site of Koobi Fora, headquarters of the archaeologists from the Museum of Nairobi. It is the site where the famous Cranium 1470, remains of the earliest known *Homo habilis*, was found.

To the southeast, the chief settlement is called Loyangalani, which can be roughly translated as "wooded place flourishing by the waterside". Perhaps the Turkana have a keen sense of irony. Or maybe the area seems lush by Turkana standards. From here, fishing expeditions are organized in pursuit of the enormous Nile perch, some of which weigh more than 100 kg (250 lb).

Don't be tempted to cool off in the lake: Turkana boasts the largest crocodile population in the whole of Africa—12,000 at the last count. From Lake Turkana Fishing Lodge, built on a promontory of the dried-out Ferguson's Gulf (centre-west), you can hire a boat to visit the usual hatching grounds of these reptiles—the greenish waters of the three crater lakes of Central Island.

Marsabit

Directly north of Samburu, the Marsabit Reserve is an unexpected oasis on the eastern edge of the Chalbi Desert, a magnificent forest that clings to a peak rising above the surrounding desolation. Rainfall is rare, but hot air rising from the desert during the day cools at nights and forms mist that gathers until the early afternoon, providing the essential humidity.

The numerous elephant have some of the longest tusks to be seen in Africa. The wildlife is abundant, in particular cats and antelope, and along with Lake Bogoria, this is one of the few places you will see the greater kudu. Volcanic cones dot the region. Your best chance of seeing the animals is when they come to slake their thirst at the edge of the small crater lakes (*gof*). That of Lake Paradise, where the trees are draped in Spanish moss, is splendid.

THE COAST
Mombasa, Beaches, Malindi, Watamu, Gedi, Lamu

After a stay in the bush, most travellers like to spend a few days lazing by the Indian Ocean. The beaches, all of white coral and mostly fringed with coconut palms, are protected by the barrier reef which keeps sharks and large waves at bay. The shallow, turquoise waters are warm year round. A wide range of activities is available for those who need to be on the move. The diving is fantastic, but if you don't want to get wet, you can explore the coral and observe the tropical fish from the shelter of a glass-bottomed boat. Deep-sea fishing is extremely popular and practised all along the coast.

Apart from offering the simple pleasures of relaxation, this part of Kenya is rich in history. Down the centuries, the boats of all the peoples living around the Indian Ocean have called in here. The Shirazis from the Persian Gulf established the first trading links, their dhows ploughing through the waters from India to Arabia and Africa, at the whim of the monsoon winds billowing their lateen sails. Cargos of precious woods and ivory—not to mention slaves—brought wealth to the East African coast until the dawn of the 20th century. Numerous Swahili cities were born of the marriage between Arabia and the Dark Continent, some of which still thrive, while others are reduced to haunting ruins.

Mombasa

At midday, a torrid heat crushes the streets beneath a leaden sky. You sense an excitement, a musical quality in the way people talk and move. In the heart of the old town, the craftsmen beat out brass fittings for elaborately carved chests, their rhythmic hammering marking the passing of time. Murmured conversations filter through heavy, sculpted doors, while odours of perfume, dust, coffee and camphorwood hang in the air. The muezzin's call to prayer resounds through the tropical torpor and brings the people out into the alleyways. Nightfall is salvation, warm and luminous, bathed in moonlight and cooled by the wind in the palms.

Linked by causeways and bridges to Kenya's east coast, what Winston Churchill in 1908 called "the gate of Africa" has been greatly modernized. He found Mombasa "alluring, even delicious", but it has always had a sleazy side, too—though Daniel Arap Moi has given it the status of city and started cleaning it up.

There are plenty of tough sailor spots where only the brave should go, but you will find plenty to keep you busy, even when you have finished shopping for silks and cinnamon, photographed the fake tusks spanning Moi Avenue and visited Fort Jesus.

As in centuries past, vessels sail into the Old Harbour from India, Arabia and the Persian Gulf, laden with carpets, silverware, spices and dates. Every April they make the return journey home with cargoes of mangrove timber, ghee, limes, animal skins and ivory. Many traders have stayed behind to give Mombasa a rich and handsome mixture of Arab and Asian peoples.

City Centre

A huge double arch formed by four tusks of sheet-metal spans Moi Avenue as a welcoming gateway for visitors coming into town from Kilindini Harbour. This symbol of the wealth and wastes of Africa was erected in honour of the visit of Princess Margaret in 1956, though the original was of wood. Nearby, Uhuru (Freedom) Fountain is built in the shape of the African continent. The Tourist Information Bureau is on hand with brochures and maps. After the crossroads, Moi Avenue becomes Nkrumah Road and reaches the shore near Fort Jesus.

THE MYTHICAL UNICORN

Local folklore has it that the oryx, a graceful antelope with long, fine horns, gave rise to the legend of the unicorn. Seen from the side, its straight horns do in fact appear as one. Pliny the Elder, in the 1st century AD, referred to the unicorn in his *Natural History* in 37 volumes, explaining that the animal lived in central Africa. In medieval Europe, the unicorn was considered as a symbol of purity.

Fort Jesus

This huge, squat building commanding the entry to Mombasa's Old Port was erected in 1593 by the Portuguese and fell to the Omani Arabs in 1968. The British used it as a prison until 1958. Set on a coral ridge with foundations of solid coral rock, it proved impregnable to conventional assault—invaders had to resort to guile and bribery to take it. Today's ground plan remains largely unchanged from that designed by Italian architect Giovanni Battista Cairato for the first Portuguese captain of Mombasa. You can still see the layout of barracks, chapel, water cistern and well, guard rooms, residences for priests and governor, and a storeroom for gunpowder.

During the Arab conquest, the powder magazine was the scene of one of history's recurring acts of mad heroism: a Portuguese officer told the Arabs the storeroom held the garrison's gold treasure, led Arab soldiers to collect it and blew them and himself to smithereens. The cannon in the courtyard are English 18th- and 19th-century naval guns brought here in 1837.

A Portuguese sailor of the 17th century has left an amusing graffiti scribbled on one of the barrack-room walls. A heart pierced by an arrow tells an immortal tale of maritime love. Nowadays the fort houses a good museum with a display of objects tracing the coast's long and colourful history, including a collection of Chinese, Persian and Portuguese ceramics, together with objects gleaned from archaeological sites along the coast and from the wreck of the *Santo Antonio de Tanna*, a galleon sunk during the siege of 1697.

The Old Town

Just north of the fort and overlooking the old harbour, where a few travel-weary dhows sometimes still lie at anchor, a tangled skein of lanes forms the old town. The winding streets are lined with old Arab houses, shutters closed to the noise and heat. Some have handsome balconies and doors finely carved in the Arab style, with the best of their dwindling number to be found on Samburu and Ndia Kun roads. Craftsmen in brass and wood can be seen at work near Mandhry Mosque, the city's oldest, built in 1570. Silk, spice and perfume merchants offer their wares from makeshift stalls, along with some shadier hustlers of gold, ivory and carved horn. Craftsmen working in copper and leather may be seen around Government Square.

The narrow passage of Leven Steps leads down to the old harbour. A dozen or so dhows preserve the memory of the graceful wind-driven craft that once plied in their hundreds between Mombasa and the Gulf. Today the large lateen sails are supplemented by motors, but they still run before the *kaskazi* (northeast monsoon) to make the voyage down.

The perfumes wafting up from the Indian shop on Leven Steps come from Arabia and Kashmir—perhaps brought back from the Orient by one of these creaky old boats. You can't miss the shop: there's an immense Portuguese wine jar outside.

The dhow careening yard is a little further north and less well known. When the tide is right you can walk out on the natural coral rock "floor", under the hulls of the boats.

Further Afield

Away from the old town, visit the Hindu temples. The one on Haile Selassie Road has a coloured door, while a dome signals that on Nkrumah Road. More recent (1963), the Jain Temple on Salim Road is built in traditional style with an exuberant white exterior. Practically next door is Mackinnon's Market, and while you are in the neighbourhood you might venture to the spice shops at the top of Langoni Road. One block further north, Biashara Street is the place to buy *kangas* or *kikois*, printed cotton fabrics that make brilliant, comfortable pareos, in addition to magic charms and medicinal plants with mysterious powers.

At the town's northern exit, beyond Makupa Causeway on the road to the airport, you can see the Wakamba woodcarvers at work in airy workshops beneath thatched roofs. They belong to a cooperative which has a shop on the spot.

The Banburi Quarry Nature Trail, on the Malindi road, makes a pleasant walk. Cape eland, oryx, buffalo and many species of bird live in freedom in this park, set up close to town. Mamba village at Nyali, a little further, is a gigantic crocodile farm.

Beaches

If the safari is Kenya's number one attraction, the beaches come a close second. The welcoming shores of the Indian Ocean, just a pebble's throw from Mombasa, are ideal for a few days of sunning and relaxing.

South Coast

The Likoni ferry from Mombasa harbour sails to the mainland and the southern coast, where several beaches lie along a 40-km (25-mile) stretch, first Shelly, then Tiwi. At low tide you can walk out to the coral reef. The diving is excellent around Sand Island, a sandbank just breaking the surface of the water. You only re-

---

THE LOST ISLAND

Very rarely visited because it's relatively difficult to reach, the little island of Wasini, off Shimoni, is a living museum of Swahili society. The only way to get there is by dhow. The island has no cars, no roads, no electricity. Coral houses with thatched roofs, the *bui-bui* (veils) of the women and *kanzu* (sarongs) of the men, over-burdened donkeys and fishing nets drying in the sun take you back to another world where time is measured only by the tides.

Fabrics billowing in the breeze on a Mombasa beach.

quire a simple mask to see a first-class underwater display. A little further (45 minutes by ferry) Diani Beach is the most popular along the south coast, easily voted the most beautiful, but also the most developed. In general its many hotels are well integrated into the landscape, surrounded by forest. They rent out all the equipment you will need for exploring the seabed. Diani's landmark is a 500-year-old baobab, 20 m (65 ft) in circumference, near the Tradewinds Hotel.

To the north, the 15th-century Kongo Mosque, still in use, is worth a visit. The southern end of Diani has retained its authenticity; in the afternoons the fishermen return, some on board *ngalawas*—outrigger canoes—and some on frail craft tossing on the waves. Small shark, barracuda and crayfish are the usual catch.

From the Pemba Channel Fishing Club (located in the direction of the Tanzanian frontier at Shimoni), enthusiasts of deep-sea fishing can go after marlin between mid-August and mid-April.

For a refreshing break from the beach routine, visit the charming little game reserve at Shimba Hills. On the wooded plateau you can take a cool, escorted stroll— no lions here—among splendid

BEACHES • MALINDI

> **A CUMBERSOME GIFT**
>
> At the beginning of the 15th century, a Chinese expedition visited the coast and received a giraffe as a token of esteem from the Sultan of Malindi to the Emperor of China. No doubt overwhelmed, he reciprocated by dispatching an ambassadorial fleet of 62 ships escorted by 37,000 men.

sable antelopes with scimitar-shaped horns, rare in Kenya. The males have handsome coats of reddish black while the females are more modestly clad in chestnut-brown. From the treehouse at Shimba Hills Lodge, you can observe elephant and perhaps even a few leopard, coming to drink at the watering-hole.

North Coast

To reach the northern beaches, take the new Nyali Bridge to the mainland. Off to the right lies English Point, site of a monument to German explorer Ludwig Krapf who charted the Kenyan interior on behalf of the British Church Missionary Society.

Nyali Beach and its beautiful neighbour Mombasa Beach are fringed with coconut palms. Beyond lie the beaches of Kenyatta-Bamburi and Shanzu, more steeply sloped and thus permitting bathing at low tide. Further north at Mtwapa Creek, you can wander round the well-preserved ruins of a small Arab town called Jumba La Mtwana (Home of the Slave-Master). A pleasant, shady town, it has two mosques, one of which is slowly but surely sliding into the sea.

Even further north, gleaming beaches lie beneath the shade of palms: Kikambala, Vipingo and Takaungu. They are fairly quiet resorts, and the water is often choked with masses of seaweed, making them less attractive for swimming.

Malindi

This is a lazy, unashamedly hedonistic beach resort whose main attractions are its dazzling white sandy beaches. The energetic say fishing here is excellent—barracuda, tuna and marlin—but do it early, before the heat of the day sets in.

Malindi had a brief spell of activity in the 16th century, when the local sheikh was rewarded with Portuguese trading concessions as thanks for his hospitality to explorer Vasco da Gama in 1498. That moment of glory is commemorated with a monument on the cliffs out on the promontory at the southern end of Malindi harbour. The Padráo, or Cross of Vasco da Gama, bearing the Portuguese coat of arms, is

MALINDI • WATAMU

one of the few authentic Portuguese relics left on the coast, along with the remains of a church that harbours memories of a visit by Saint Francis Xavier on his way to the Indies.

Another famous name connected with Malindi is that of Ernest Hemingway, who came here in the 1930s to fish for marlin off Palm Beach. Since then, an unprecedented tourist boom has launched the construction of luxury hotels all along the shore.

Prefer the southern beaches: those to the north are spoiled by muddy waters brought down by the Sabaki River, whereas south of the resort, the sea is crystal clear. Silversands Bay, gateway to Malindi Marine National Park, is absolutely perfect. The marine park's fragile natural beauties are a joy for scuba-divers and snorkellers, with an astonishing variety of fish and coral (especially brain coral).

Ask to be taken to the Coral Gardens at the southern end of North Reef. Here the water is shallow and translucent. Glass-bottomed boats are available for hire if you want to keep dry. Landlubbers are well catered for, too, with golf and tennis facilities. And for night-owls, Malindi has several discothèques and even a casino.

Watamu

Continuing the Malindi beaches towards the south, Watamu is a relatively recent resort built around Tortoise Bay (named after a small tortoise-shaped island). There are in fact three successive bays, all with fine, dazzlingly white sand and shaded by coconut palms.

Diving in the marine reserve is even better than at Malindi. All the necessary equipment, as well as glass-bottomed boats, are available for hire. Watamu is well known for its deep-sea fishing, too: marlin frequent the neighbouring waters all through the winter.

5

THE FIVE MOST BEAUTIFUL BEACHES

From Somalia to Tanzania, the waves of the Indian Ocean roll up on a shoreline stretching for 500 km (300 miles). From north to south, the most beautiful strands are **Shela** (Lamu), **Silversands** (Malindi), **Watamu**, **Mombasa Beach** and **Diani**. White sands, limpid waters and palm trees guaranteed.

Gedi

Close to Watamu, the abandoned ruins of this old Swahili town are the best-preserved in all Kenya. Their history, however, remains an enigma. It would appear that the settlement dawned in the 13th century, only to vanish for no apparent reason in the 17th—perhaps because of invasion by a hostile tribe, or maybe the water supply dried up. It's also strange that Gedi has never been mentioned by a single trader or passing sailor, though that could be explained by the fact that the town was built inland, invisible from the shore.

At the end of the day, when the light of the setting sun glances off the stones, the ruins take on a magical aura. The great mosque, the palace, and the houses huddled in between seem to come back to life for an instant. The old city is protected by two encircling walls and shrouded in forest, which rings with the shrieks of monkeys. The site is open until 6 p.m. Near the entrance, a small museum displays various archaeological finds.

Lamu

Far to the north, the small island of Lamu is the living legacy of a civilization centuries old. As in Zanzibar, the Swahili heritage has survived the passing of time. Lamu is in fact the name of the town, the island and the archipelago, the three forming an inseparable whole.

The capital, with its tangle of narrow streets, its mosques and fort, exudes an old-fashioned, oriental charm. It is accessible only by boat: aircraft have to land on a neighbouring island. The magnificent beaches are lined with dhows, still built in the traditional way by the villagers of Matondoni. Manda, Paté and other islands still hold memories of a glorious past.

The Old Town

Its coral walls rise at the very edge of the ocean. Behind the arcades and columns of the seafront, a network of tiny squares and winding lanes enmeshes the stone façades of beautiful houses. Finely worked lintels display two types of motif: interwoven floral elements borrowed from the Indian artistic tradition, and geometrical *bajun* designs, named after the local fishermen. Great carved doors, typical of the old Arab trading posts in Africa, creak open to reveal courtyards and flower-filled gardens.

In the shadow of the old fort (which houses an aquarium, a museum of natural history and the library), all the produce of the island and the mainland is heaped high on the market stalls in joyous disorder. The ceaseless

Who knows the mysteries concealed behind Gedi's walls?

hubbub dims only when the muezzin's cry rings through the air. The city has no less than 29 mosques, from Msikiti wa Pwani, the oldest, built at the end of the 14th century, to the grand new Riyadha Mosque. Every year, the great Maulidi festival celebrates the birth of the Prophet, when pilgrims flood in from all over Kenya and elsewhere. A local saying has it that to participate in the Maulidi festival is worth half a pilgrimage to Mecca.

For more insight into the history and culture of Lamu, visit the museum, housed in the old British consular residence near the harbour, or its annex, the Swahili House Museum somewhere in the middle of the maze of Old Town streets, near the Yumbe Hotel.

Lamu Island

A 15-minute dhow trip takes you to Shela, south of Lamu town. A mosque and minaret loom over the hamlet, which has been developed to cope with the increase in tourism. The day's activities comprise windsurfing, fishing or simply lazing beneath the palm trees on a superlative beach.

A fleet of dhows bob at anchor in Lamu's harbour, but the only people still capable of building them in the traditional way are all

at Matondi village. The biggest dhows, *jahazi*, are crafted in boatyards by the edge of the mangrove swamp hemming the western shore. You can go there by dhow or on foot, along a dusty path which takes you through coconut groves and sparse crops.

Lamu Archipelago

To savour Lamu's atmosphere of times past, nothing can beat sailing round the islands in a dhow, at the whim of the winds and the tides. All the larger islands were important trading centres, many of the towns now reduced to ruins. Some of them, according to the ancient chronicle of Paté, flourished a thousand years ago.

Manda is separated from Lamu by a narrow channel endlessly plied by craft of all kinds. In the southeast of the island, the 17th-century ruins of Takwa stand on a peninsula. All the houses, not to mention the mosque, are carefully aligned to face northwest, the direction of Mecca.

In the 14th century, until its port silted up, the sultanate of Paté commanded the East African coast from Kilwa (Tanzania) in the south to Washiekh (Somalia) in the north. Paté town was celebrated for gold and silver jewellery and its vibrantly illuminated copies of the Koran. Today, you can visit the ruins of several settlements: Paté itself; Siyu, once a great centre of Islamic learning (the fort is very well restored); and Shanga, one of the very first Swahili settlements.

SWAHILI

A mixture of one-third Arabic (for the vocabulary) and two-thirds Bantu (for everything else), Swahili is a sort of *lingua franca*, the common thread which binds together the past of all the lands around the Indian Ocean. A few words of Portuguese have been incorporated, while the word Swahili itself comes from the Arabic word for the coast—sahel.

At first only a spoken language, Swahili was written in Arabic characters then transcribed phonetically into the Latin alphabet by the English missionaries; consequently it is easy to pronounce. Words are formed by adding a prefix to a basic root to indicate singular and plural, verb tenses, adjectives and adverbs. *Mtoto*, for instance, is a child, *watoto*, children. The prefix *ki-* is used to indicate inanimate objects, which is why Swahili in Swahili is *Kiswahili*.

It's worth giving the dhows a very close inspection.

Cultural Notes

Dhow

For more than 2,000 years, the East African coast has been visited by traders. Well before the beginning of the Christian era, Phoenicians and Greeks frequented these shores. Arab seafarers, coming from the Persian Gulf and the Arabian peninsula, began trading here in the 8th century—perhaps even earlier. Their great ocean-going dhows reached Africa driven by the northeast monsoon winds, which blow from November to April. Business concluded, they set sail for home at the mercy of the inverse monsoon between June and October. Today, there remain very few of the big dhows making the great journey to Arabia, and even fewer venture as far as India. Copra and cotton, not to mention contraband, have replaced the old cargoes of ivory, precious woods and slaves.

Elmolo People

At the edge of Lake Turkana—the Jade Sea of the northern desert—lives the smallest tribe in Kenya, perhaps in all of Africa. Of Cushitic origin, the Elmolo people today number only a few hundred, though the population has been increasing since they started intermarrying with the Samburu. Unlike the other tribes of the region, which are mainly pastoralists, they live from fishing. Another source of revenue is the fees they charge tourists for taking their photos. No-one can explain where they came from, nor why they settled on these torrid shores.

Flying Doctors

Inaugurated in Kenya at the end of the 1950s, the Flying Doctor Foundation offers its services free of charge, even in the most isolated parts of the country. From their headquarters at Nairobi's Wilson Airport, the doctors maintain radio contact with more than 120 operators scattered all over the national territory. They deal mainly with emergency situations, but more and more long-term projects have been initiated in recent years. The foundation has been so successful that it now operates in several neighbouring countries.

Indians

Brought to Kenya to work as labourers during the construction of the railway from Mombasa to Lake Victoria, the Indians (mostly from Gujarat and the Punjab) gradually became an indispensable factor in the national economy. Driven from the countryside after independence by the emergence of a class of Kikuyu entrepreneurs, they moved into the towns, where today they dominate the retail and property markets. Numbering about 150,000, the Indian community is very active and still keeps many of its traditions alive.

Kanga, kikoi and co.

An African cotton cloth, the *kanga* is printed with brightly coloured patterns, generally accompanied by Swahili proverbs. The lengths of fabric are always sold in pairs: one is worn by a woman as a sort of sarong, the other is used as a sling to carry her baby on her back. The heavier weave *kikoi*, to be found in villages along the coast, is worn by men knotted round the waist like a skirt. Muslim men dress in a white garment called the *kanzu*. Swahili women wear the *bui-bui*, an enormous black veil that swathes them from head to ankles.

Makonde

The Makonde ebony carvings, although originating in southern Tanzania, are today found all over East Africa. The high quality of the finish and the fact that they are one of the rare forms of sculptural art in the region make them very collectable objects. There are two types: modern, slender carvings that seem inspired by Giacometti's elongated forms, and traditional designs, more typically African in shape and execution.

Tribe

Although urban Kenya—and by extension the rest of the country—is increasingly adopting western values, the notion of the tribe has not yet disappeared. On the contrary, everyone refers to his tribe as an important facet of his identity. Most people speak a tribal language as well as the national Swahili. The majority of ethnic groups still practice circumcision as a rite of passage to adult life, and some—despite the law—have not yet abandoned excision. Marriage takes place primarily within the same tribe.

Women

In Kenya as elsewhere in Africa, it's the women who do all the work. They tend the fields, but do not have the right to own land. They are responsible for collecting wood, the main fuel, for fetching water and for looking after the children. The country has one of the highest birthrates in the world, with an average of 6.8 children per woman. Traditionally, divorce is not allowed. The exception is the Luo tribe, where divorce can be granted to a woman, but for one reason only—if her husband ever dares to set foot in the kitchen.

Dining Out

The daily Kenyan fare—like African cooking in general—does not rate very high in the gourmet guides. However, the starchy staples are improved by the use of spices, and the fruit and vegetables are fresh and varied. Year-round, there's plenty of choice.

Though food in Nairobi hotels and some of the game lodges may be blandly "English", Mombasa and other coastal resorts benefit from the Indian Ocean's succulent spiny lobster, shrimps and prawns—astoundingly cheap by European standards. The Arab influence and contact with the cosmopolitan seafarers of the Indian Ocean is reflected in the richness of Swahili dishes, where coconut mingles with the exotic flavours of saffron and turmeric. Try lunch or dinner in one of the numerous ethnic restaurants of Mombasa or Nairobi. Indian restaurants are the most widespread (some of them vegetarian), but you will also find Italian, Chinese and even French or Japanese.

Breakfast

Hotels in towns and lodges in the bush propose a breakfast buffet featuring cereals, fried eggs, toast, fruit juice, pastries—in other words, everything a hungry tourist could wish for. A refreshing local touch is the systematic inclusion of fresh pineapple and papaya. Kenyans themselves start the day by indulging in their fondness for *mandazi*, a starchy fritter.

On the menu

Buffet tables are set with big, appetizing bowls of mixed salads and raw vegetable dishes as starters. The usual main course is meat—beef, goat or mutton.

African food is an acquired taste but worth trying at least once. The national dish, also spreading to neighbouring countries, is *nyama choma*, barbecued meat cut into small pieces and accompanied by *matoke*—plantains—or by *ugali*—a porridge-like corn mush, left to set solid then served in chunks. Very popular among the wealthier Kenyans as well as expats, the best *nyama choma* offer a range of meats from beef to the more exotic impala by way of giraffe (best avoided as it is tasteless).

If you are tempted to try everyday Kenyan food, ask for *irio*, a Kikuyu dish that has become popular all over the country. It's a mixture of peas mashed with potato (and sometimes sweet potato) and sweetcorn. *Sukuma wiki na nyama* is a sauté of spinach with meat. On the coast, you'll find *kuku wakupaka*, a spicy chicken dish from Lamu, but you won't have to complain if the chicken is a bit stringy.

Fish and seafood
Kenyan food makes its entry into the realms of gastronomy along the coast—at least for those who like fish. Apart from the delicious crayfish, shrimp and lobster, swordfish and moonfish are worth trying, and you might well be tempted by a meaty shark steak. These are all at their best when simply grilled and served with, at most, a butter sauce.

Elsewhere in the country you will find the king of African freshwater fish, the tilapia.

What's for pudding?
Yoghurt is readily available. English specialities—apple tart, fruit cake, pineapple cake and muffins feature on most menus. The most refreshing dessert is fruit, grown all over the country. You'll have seen in the markets the luscious piles of mangoes (the red ones are the best), papayas, pineapples (deliciously sweet), guavas, melons, watermelons and the whole gamut of citrus fruit. Not to mention strawberries, now exported to Europe.

Worthy French and English cheeses (of local manufacture) are to be found, but you'll have to ask.

Drinks
Wines are imported from Europe and Australia, but it is worth trying those from South Africa, which now enjoy a worldwide reputation. You'll also find wines from Zimbabwe and even Ethiopia. A few drinkable whites are produced in the Lake Naivasha vineyards, and if you're not too demanding you might like to try some of the local wines made from fruit (the papaya is unusual, to say the least).

But the most popular thirst-quencher by far is beer, available in three brands, White Cap, Tusker and Pilsner, with little to distinguish one from the other. Strangely, most Kenyans seem to prefer it at room temperature, but you can always ask for it chilled. Soft drinks and fresh fruit juices are available in the towns; passion fruit juice is very good. Fresh chilled coconut milk, *maduf*, is a good cool pick-me-up in the heat of the day.

Shopping

The most attractive souvenirs are handmade items. Prices are in general fairly low, but be vigilant all the same: it's usual practice to haggle in the markets. Check whatever you buy for quality.

Where?

It won't take you long to discover that street vendors are numerous and pesky. The goods they offer are not usually of the best quality. In Nairobi, do your shopping at the stalls behind the mosque or in the municipal market (entrance at the junction of Muindi Mbingo and Market streets), where there's a profusion of small shops overlooking the fruit and vegetable stalls. The capital also has an increasing number of galleries that specialize in superior quality goods, some of which come from other African countries. Prices are fixed, which is a boon if bargaining embarrasses you.

Wood

Animals feature in most carvings, in all sizes from tiny key-rings to giraffes as tall as a basketball player. Whatever the size, they make pleasing gifts for a child. "Masai" sculptures—elongated shapes representing herdsmen, singly or in groups—unite European art and African inspiration. Known as *Makonde*, these are modern versions of traditional Tanzanian sculpture. You can be sure that the Makonde sold in galleries is genuine ebony; elsewhere you might be fobbed off with inferior, light-coloured woods stained dark with boot polish. Along the coast, look out for camphorwood chests in the old town of Mombasa, or the magnificent carved wooden trays from Lamu.

Tribal Art

Souvenirs with a tribal theme can be found everywhere: Masai bead jewellery, spears and shields, carved calabashes. If you are tempted, visit African Heritage, a gallery on Kenyatta Avenue in Nairobi where everything is of very high quality.

Soapstone

The only soapstone quarry in the country is located at the village of Tabaka near Lake Victoria. It is similar to the stone carved by Inuit craftsmen in Canada, in

SHOPPING

Fruit and veg lined up neatly in Nairobi's market.

cream shades varying from pinkish to greyish. The carvings are very beautiful: human and animal figures, vases, jewellery boxes, candlesticks, sometimes coloured black and etched so the base colour shows through. The disadvantage of soapstone is that it weighs a ton.

Fabrics

African cottons, printed with motifs of animals or African proverbs, are both inexpensive and easy to transport. You can have them cut to size on the spot if you so wish. Both Nairobi and Mombasa have a Biashara Street specializing in these fabrics. You can also find batiks depicting safari scenes.

Leather Goods

The only item available in this category is the *kiondo*, an all-purpose basket woven from sisal and trimmed with leather. They are attractively striped in bright colours, but only the most expensive are made to last.

Gemstones

Semi-precious stones such as ruby, amethyst, jasper, malachite and agate are available in every jeweller's, and you'll also find violet tanzanite and emerald-like tsavorite.

Sports

From the shores of the Indian Ocean to the highest peaks of Africa, Kenya will delight mountaineers and watersports enthusiasts alike. There is no lack of possibilities: from the most energetic—rafting, climbing and even parachuting—to the simplest of seaside leisure activities.

Diving
The coral reef which runs along the coast opens up prospects of wonderful snorkelling opportunities—and keeps out the sharks. Although visibility is sometimes reduced by the plankton, there are always plenty of beautifully coloured fish. The corals are magnificent, particularly off Shimoni and around Wasini Island (Kisite Marine Park) and in the marine reserve near Watamu and Malindi. From Lamu, take a dhow to the island of Manda Toto for a spectacular display. Glass-bottom boats can be hired at hotels and on the beach; they usually have snorkelling gear on board. Scuba-diving equipment can also be hired.

Windsurfing
Most hotels both north and south of Mombasa and Malindi have surfboards for hire at reasonable prices. Conditions are good all year round: the waters are protected by the barrier reef and the breeze blows steadily from the sea.

Fishing
Deep-sea fishing has been popular in Kenya for several years now—for barracuda, kingfish, sailfish and shark, but especially marlin. The Pemba Channel Fishing Club is reputed to have the best fishing grounds along the entire East African coast, but you can also enjoy expeditions from the resorts of Malindi, Watamu and Diani. The season lasts from November to March.

In the interior, specialized tour operators offer fishing for trout in the rivers of the Aberdares, tilapia in Lake Victoria (by seaplane) or gigantic Nile perch in Lake Turkana.

Walking/Climbing
Whereas Kilimanjaro can only be climbed from Tanzania (allow about a week for the round trip),

SPORTS

Spectator sport with a difference—drifting over the savannah in a balloon.

Mount Kenya offers numerous possibilities for hikers. Lenana Point is accessible to reasonably fit ramblers, while the higher peaks (Batian and Nelion) should be attempted only by experienced mountain climbers. Mount Elgon also provides superb walking country.

Rafting

Rafting is still in its infancy in Kenya, but you can, for example, descend the River Athi near Nairobi. It boasts several miles of rapids interspersed with calm stretches.

You can also raft down the River Tsavo, gentler, with occasional opportunities for observing the wildlife, thus doubling the pleasures of the trip.

Golf

In Kenya you'll find some of the best golf courses in the whole continent: the Windsor Golf and Country Club, a championship course close to Nairobi, is particularly appealing. Most of the courses are located on the high plateaux, where it's pleasant to play all year round (except during the rainy season). Don't be surprised if your drive mysteriously increases by several yards without any extra effort on your part —it's all thanks to the altitude.

The Hard Facts

Airports

Most international flights land at Nairobi's Jomo Kenyatta Airport (NBO), 16 km (10 miles) south-east of the city. There you will find a Tourist Office, several car-hire desks, a 24-hour bank and bureau de change, a post office and a bar, and a duty-free shop for outgoing passengers. Internal flights leave from the small Wilson Airport nearer to the city centre.

Mombasa (Moi International, MBA), the second airport of Kenya, is 13 km (8 miles) west of the city. It handles a growing number of international flights. Airport facilities include car-hire services, a bank open from 5 a.m. to 2 p.m., bar and Tourist Information Office.

Taxis are available at both airports; agree on the fare before getting inside. The British-style black cabs and state-controlled Kenatco taxis work to a fixed rate. Airlines also provide regular bus transport to terminals in the city centres. Most tourist hotels have minibuses to pick up guests at the airport.

Banks

Banks open Monday to Friday, 8.30 or 9 a.m. to 3 p.m; some stay open longer Thursdays, and some open Saturdays from. 9 to 11 a.m..

You can change money and travellers cheques in the better hotels, but at an unfavourable exchange rate. Credit cards are accepted by all the big hotels and airlines, and increasingly by smaller shops. You can also use them to obtain money from cash-point machines as long as you know your PIN number.

Don't forget to keep a little local currency for the departure tax, payable in cash at the airport. As procedures tend to be slow, arrive at the airport well in time for your return flight.

Climate

As a general rule, the coast is hot and sunny for most of the year, whereas the high plateaux (Nairobi) have a more temperate climate—you'll need a sweater for the summer evenings.

The months of January to March are the driest and hottest. They are followed by the rainy season which, some years, can last until May or even the beginning of June. The summer is cloudy and cool in Nairobi and less hot on the coast. September is generally sunny and pleasant. November is typically showery.

Clothing

Depending on the time of year and whether you are going to the coast, to Nairobi or to the game reserves, you will need a fairly comprehensive wardrobe (including warm clothing for nighttime). Cotton garments are the most appropriate and the most comfortable everywhere. On safari it is advisable to wear trousers and stout, lace-up shoes.

Communications

The Kenyan postal service is fairly reliable. Letters take an average of four to seven days to reach Europe. Faxes can be sent from the main post offices in the large towns. The telephone works reasonably well. You can place calls from phone centres or from international telephone boxes. The outgoing international code is 000. For operator-assistance dial 0196. Phone cards are available. If you place calls from your hotel room, expect to pay a surcharge. The mobile phone network is GSM 900. Internet cafés can be found in cities and hotels.

Currency

The Shilling (Sh) is divided into 100 cents (c). The exchange rate fluctuates rapidly. There are banknotes of 50, 100, 200, 500 and 1,000 Sh. The most frequently used coins are 1, 5, 10, 20 and 40 Sh.

The black market has essentially ceased to exist since the liberalization of exchange controls; if someone offers you a miraculous deal in the street, refuse.

Electricity

Kenya uses the British 240-volt system and 3-pin plugs. Electrical goods designed for 220 volts can be used safely.

Emergencies

In case of theft, go to the nearest police station to obtain the official declaration required by your insurance company. If you lose your passport, go immediately to the nearest consulate: the consular staff are familiar with this problem and can help you out if necessary.

British High Commission
  PO Box 30465
  Upper Hill Road, Nairobi
  Tel. 20 2844 000
  Fax 20 2844 239
  www.britishhighcommission.gov.uk/kenya
There are British consulates in Mombasa and Malindi

Canadian High Commission
  Limuru Road, Gigiri (street)
  P.O.Box 1013,
  00621 Nairobi (postal)
  Tel. 20 3663 000
  Fax 20 3663 900
  www.dfait-maeci.gc.ca/nairobi

THE HARD FACTS

US Embassy:
United Nations Avenue
Nairobi (street)
PO Box 606
Village Market
00621 Nairobi (postal)
Tel. 02 3636 000
consularnairobi@state.gov
http://nairobi.usembassy.gov/

Essentials
Practically everything is available in Nairobi, but do not forget any medication you may need. Take an insect repellent and sunblock cream. A torch (flashlight) may be useful on safari.

Formalities
Your passport must be valid for the entire length of your intended stay. If you hold a British, Canadian, Australian or US passport, you need a visa for stays up to three months (obtainable from the Consular section of the Kenyan Embassy or High Commission in your home country; allow 5 working days).

Passengers aged 16 years or over are allowed to import, duty-free, 200 cigarettes or 50 cigars or 500 g tobacco and one bottle of wine or spirits.

Health
Water served in the hotels and lodges is safe to drink; tap water is chlorinated. Avoid ice cubes and prefer bottled water.

Protection from the sun is essential. A hat, sunglasses and sunblock cream are indispensable, especially on the beaches of the Indian Ocean.

Vaccination against yellow fever is recommended if you are visiting any area outside the main cities. It is also highly advisable to follow a preventive treatment against malaria. Start the treatment before leaving home, and continue four two weeks after your return. Your doctor will advise you. The anti-malarial drug Mefloquine (sold under the brand name Lariam or Mephaquine) has been reported to have unpleasant side effects such as nausea, dizziness and vivid dreams. Chloroquine (also sold as Nivaquine, Roquine and Aralen) is not effective in Kenya.

Never swim in a river, a lake or a natural reservoir, often infected with the bilharzia parasite.

Languages
In the towns, almost everyone can speak English. In the rural areas a few words of Swahili will be appreciated. On the coast, German and to a lesser extent, Italian (at Malindi), are increasingly spoken in response to tourist pressures.

Media
The Nation is the most liberal of the daily newspapers, mostly

published in English; you will also find the *Kenya Times* and *The Standard*. In Nairobi and Mombasa, all the leading European papers can be found.

Two television channels, KBC and KTN, broadcast in English. There are also cable channels.

Opening Hours
Administrative offices are open from Monday to Friday from 8 or 8.30 a.m. until 1 p.m. and from 2 p.m. until 5 p.m. Some services close earlier on Friday afternoons. Most shops are shut at the weekend, apart from a few souvenir or food stores which stay open on Saturdays—especially in the morning.

Photography
You will find almost all types of film (prints and slides) except for high sensitivity (400 ASA and above). On safari, whenever you take pictures with a zoom or telephoto lens, it is preferable to use 200 or 400 ASA. Certain tribes will accept to be photographed, usually in exchange for a small sum of money. The Masai are more reticent than the others. Protect your equipment from the heat and dust and from the sun, and observe restrictions.

Public Holidays
On public holidays everything is closed. Holidays falling on a Sunday are observed on the following Monday.

January 1	*New Year's Day*
May 1	*Labour Day*
June 1	*Madarka Day*
October 10	*Moi Day*
October 20	*Kenyatta Day*
December 12	*Independence Day*
December 25	*Christmas Day*
December 26	*Boxing Day*

Moveable holidays are Good Friday and Easter Monday. The feast celebrating the end of Ramadan, *Id-ul-Fitr,* is also a public holiday. In addition, there are a certain number of Muslim festivals which are chiefly observed at the coast.

The dates vary from year to year as they are based on the lunar calendar. The most famous is *Maulidi*, celebrated at Lamu and attracting pilgrims from all over the Islamic world.

Safety
In town, do not wear jewellery in public and do not carry large sums of money or a handbag. Use the hotel safe for all your valuables, cameras and passports. Do not respond to any proposals which are made to you in the street. As a general rule, do not go out after dark, and certainly never after 10 p.m. And do not take any risks when on safari.

Taxis

For local transport it is advisable to take a taxi (agree on the price before setting out: there are no meters). The buses and *matatus* (minibuses) are overcrowded and the drivers are not renowned for their prudence.

Time Difference

Kenya is three hours ahead of GMT, all year round.

Tipping

Most hotel and restaurant bills include a service charge of 10 per cent. It is usual to leave an extra 10 or 20 Sh per head. Your safari guide will expect a tip of 100 to 150 Sh per day.

Toilets

There are no public toilets except at the airports and railway stations, but do not expect too high a standard. In case of need, the only possibilities are in a hotel or restaurant.

Tourist Information

Addresses of the Kenya tourist offices are listed on the inside back cover of this guide. See also the official website:
www.magicalkenya.com

Transport

The road network leaves a lot to be desired, and all long distances are best covered by air. However, the national parks and reserves (except for the largest which have landing strips) are only accessible by road. The usual transport is by four-wheel-drive vehicle or minibus; the tour drivers are used to coping with the pot-holed, sandy and muddy roads.

In the towns you can hire a car to explore further afield on your own, if you don't mind the expense. Charges for four-wheel-drive vehicles are particularly extravagant. The minimum age for car rental varies from 23 to 25 years.

Kenya Railways have a night service between Nairobi and Mombasa. It is advisable to book seats on the express. Other lines go west, but the trains are so slow and the nighttime timetable is so inconvenient that they are not worth considering.

TANZANIA

TANZANIA

Beneath the Roof of Africa

Mainland Tanzania is breathtakingly immense and beautiful. The largest country in East Africa, it was the first to gain independence from the European colonial powers. It's a land that cries out for superlatives, since it contains the highest mountain in the whole continent—the legendary Kilimanjaro, "roof of Africa, eternally capped with snow—and, in the heart of the Rift Valley, the earth's second-deepest lake.

Tanzania also has the highest concentration of wildlife in the world, which it protects in extensive national parks. The Ngorongoro crater alone—the world's largest unbroken caldera—is a veritable Noah's ark, harbouring every species of animal in Africa except the giraffe, whose long legs can't cope with the crater's steep slopes. Elsewhere in Tanzania, however, these gangly creatures are such a common sight that the country is sometimes known as the "land of the giraffe".

A string of ancient volcanoes marks the frontier with Kenya, to the north. Most of Tanzania's national parks are concentrated in this part of the country, though there are also huge reserves in the south, untouched as yet by tourism. For political reasons, Tanzania receives only a quarter as many visitors as Kenya. The country was long closed to foreigners, and its tourist infrastructure is still being developed.

As if turning their backs on the emptiness of the hinterland, the population of some 25 million live mainly around the country's fringes. Altogether, more than 120 ethnic tribes live scattered over the forested mountains and great plateaux. Dodoma, the new administrative capital in the centre of the country, seems somewhat lost in the immensity of the landscape, unable to compete with Dar es-Salaam. Clinging to the shores of the Indian Ocean, the latter is universally recognized as the unofficial capital. The streets of its older districts are pervaded by an exotic oriental atmosphere, where India and Arabia rub shoulders with Africa.

The name Tanzania melds the "tan" of Tanganyika with the "zan" of the offshore island of Zanzibar, separated from the mainland by a 37-km (23-mile) channel. Many people imagine that they are two different countries, but the two entities were united in 1964 (along with Zanzibar's sister island Pemba and

For the Masai, fashion accessories speak a symbolic language.

some other small islets). Once the trading centre for the whole of East Africa, Zanzibar is part of a coral reef stretching down Africa's Indian Ocean coast. As early as the 10th century, Persian merchants migrated here. Portuguese influence secured a foothold with Vasco da Gama's visit in 1499. Later came the Germans and the British. The main language is Swahili, a tongue belonging to the Bantu family that is strongly tinged with Arabic, but English is also fairly commonly understood. When they settled here, the Persians introduced Islam, which most Zanzibaris still practise strictly.

Countless memories, at once romantic and cruel, crowd into this small island. Over the centuries it shipped out fortunes in ivory, rhinoceros horn, gold, copper and spices. But to its infamy, it also provided the market for the great slave route which ran from Ujiji on Lake Tanganyika to the coastal port of Bagamoyo. Dr David Livingstone, the 19th-century Scottish missionary-explorer who fought so hard against slavery, made Zanzibar the base camp for his last expedition.

Zanzibar Town, and the splendid, squalid streets of its Stone Town heart, is set on a small peninsula, once cut off by a creek. There's usually a sea breeze to temper the sizzling heat. The island has several fine, white sand beaches. Inland, the smoke from fires drying coconuts for copra hangs hazily over the countryside, and bananas thrive in the red clay soil. So do spice trees: cloves were planted on the order of Seyyid Said bin Sultan, the ruler of Oman, who held court on the island in the 19th century.

From the heady fragrance of the spice groves to the restful sight of a dhow's triangular sails billowing in the wind, the charms of Zanzibar make it one of Africa's most fascinating islands.

A Brief History

Prehistory	The excavations of Louis and Mary Leakey in the Olduvai Gorge in 1959 bring to light the "Nutcracker Man"—a virtually complete hominid cranium 1.8 million years old, later named *Australopithecus boisei*. Anthropologists are fairly certain today that the Rift Valley is the cradle of humanity.
8th–10th centuries	Arab trading posts are established along the coast of East Africa. Islam is introduced.

13th–15th centuries	Settlers from the Persian Gulf (Shirazis) gradually colonize the region. They integrate with the African population and from this union arises the Swahili culture. In 1498, Vasco de Gama rounds the Cape of Good Hope and reaches East Africa.
16th–17th centuries	The 16th and early 17th centuries are dominated by the Portuguese who seek to control the route to the Indies. Progressively, however, Moorish influence takes over and in 1698 Zanzibar and the East African coast fall into the hands of the Omani Arabs, who establish several petty kingdoms.
18th century	Swahili traders penetrate the interior in search of precious commodities: white gold (ivory) and black gold (slaves). Their culture spreads all along the caravan routes.
19th century	Seyyid Said bin Sultan assumes the throne of Oman at the beginning of the century and sends his armies to the East African colonies to put an end to the strife among the cities. In 1828 he moves his capital to Zanzibar, from where he controls the entire coast. The island reaches the height of its glory with the introduction of the clove. The port becomes the greatest slave market of all Africa. The "spice island" is so prosperous that it suffers continual pirate raids. European powers begin to take an interest in Africa. In the 1870s the first missionaries, including David Livingstone, begin the fight against slavery. Abolished initially in 1873, it does not really die out until the end of the century. On January 1, 1891, Germany proclaims a protectorate over all Tanganyikan territory but subsequently cedes Zanzibar to Great Britain, which maintains the Sultanate there.
20th century	After its defeat in World War I, Germany loses Tanganyika. Great Britain is given an administrative mandate, but the country is too poor in natural resources to excite great interest. In 1961, the territory obtains its independence in a painless transition, and Julius Nyerere takes charge of the new state and directs it along a collectivist path. At the end of 1963, Zanzibar—still under British control—also becomes independent. Only one month later a bloody revolution

drives out the sultan and unification is announced: Tanganyika and Zanzibar merge to form the new Tanzania.

Nyerere finally relinquishes power in 1985. His successor, Ali Hassan Mwinyi, tries to steer Tanzania towards economic and political liberalization, but Nyerere's shadow still lies over the land. In 1993 Zanzibar causes constitutional controversy by deciding unilaterally to join the Organisation of the Islamic Conference (OIC). It later withdraws its membership. The first free elections held in October 1995 bring Benjamin William Mkapa to power. He is succeeded by Jakaya Kikwete in December 2005.

Sightseeing

Washed by the Indian Ocean, the chiefly Muslim cities of Dar es-Salaam (literally "haven of peace" in Arabic) and Zanzibar town, capital of the spice island, symbolize Tanzania's many-faceted history, which has fired the imagination of generations of adventurers. Before or after a safari, the coast is the ideal place to laze away a few days in the shade of coconut palms. Year round, the turquoise waters are temptingly warm.

Dar es-Salaam

The country's former capital Dar es-Salaam is a relatively young city. A simple fishing village in the 19th century, it started developing in 1860 when the Sultan of Zanzibar decided to turn it into a commercial port. It became the seat of the German colonial governor in 1891 and has retained its importance ever since. Today Dar es-Salaam is a metropolis of 2.5 million inhabitants and one of the rare large African cities without a shantytown.

A few faded buildings remain in the town centre, as testimony to the German presence, and dhows still tie up along the bay lined with palms and mangrove. The main commercial street is **Samora Avenue**. At its northern end, the **National Museum** is well worth a visit for its palaeontological collections which include the cranium of *Australopithecus boisei* and bones from *Homo habilis*, the sensational discoveries of the Leakey family of anthropologists. The large ethnographical section displays traditional musical instruments and crafts, weapons, Makonde sculptures and various weird objects associated with witchcraft.

Take a trip southwest of the town centre to explore the **Kariakoo** area, bounded by Mkun-

Calm waters and bobbing dhows off the coast of bustling Dar es-Salaam.

guni and Tandamuti streets; in its dazzlingly colourful market everything is sold in joyous disarray—heaps of fruit and vegetables, spices, fish, flowers. The Indian district spreads around **India Street**.

Going north out of town, you pass through the wealthy suburbs and soon reach **Oyster Bay**, Dar es-Salaam's nearest beach. The magnificent stretch of sand, as white as salt and powdery fine, is shaded by coconut fronds.

About 10 km (6 miles) from the city centre, along the Bagamoyo road, stop off at the **Village Museum**, a reconstitution of the traditional dwellings of some fifteen ethnic groups. Demonstrations of dances are organized here every weekend. The cooperative of **Mwenge**, some 3 km (less than 2 miles) to the north, produces high-quality Makonde woodcarvings.

Tanzania's main **resort area** lies a good 10 km (6 miles) further north, where the beaches of Kunduchi, Bahari and Silver Sands are just as beautiful as Oyster Bay, though the high tide sweeps in with it an unpleasant bonus of seaweed. Most of the hotels offer boat trips, some visiting the scattering of islands off shore, such as Mbudya. Don't risk walking from one hotel to another as the area is notorious for muggings. It's better to choose one beach and stay there, or take a taxi.

Some 30 km (18 miles) south of Dar es-Salaam, new amenities are fast sprouting up around **Ras Kutani Beach Resort**, a luxurious hotel complex well integrated into the landscape.

North Coast

From Dar es-Salaam to Lunga Lunga on the Kenyan border, the coast is lined with almost 300 km (180 miles) of beaches, many of them quite splendid.

Bagamoyo means "lay down the burden of your heart". The name is a story in itself and evokes part of this coastal town's tragic history. As recorded by an eyewitness, Reverend Charles New, caravans of captive slaves, from as far inland as the Lake Tanganyika region, were force-marched to the Bagamoyo Customs House, "their necks galling and jolted almost to dislocation in the prong of the rough branch by which they are secured; with heavy chains on their hands, backs smarting under frequent blows, loins lank with starvation, and tongues withered with thirst; with burdens upon their heads, and still heavier ones in their hearts". After payment of a duty of two dollars to the Sultan, they were shipped off in overloaded dhows to Zanzibar's slave market, some, reportedly, in such a state that they "met the fate of all damaged goods by being allowed to go to waste".

In the north part of town, the Catholic mission maintains a small **museum** devoted partly to the horrors of the slave trade and partly to the explorers Burton, Speke and Stanley. Livingstone's body was laid here before being taken to England for burial in Westminster Abbey.

Little is left of the old town, apart from a few once-elegant buildings dating from German colonial days. Moreover, Bagamoyo is not a particularly safe place to visit: armed gangs have been known to mug tourists as soon as they leave the streets of the centre, as well as on the beach. If, however, you are keen to visit the ruins of the little 14th-century Shirazi city of **Kaole**, 5 km (3 miles) south of town, be sure to take a taxi.

Further north, **Pangani** looks out onto a wide bay hemmed in by coral reefs and a string of beautiful sandy islets. It's fairly easy to charter a boat to visit one or two of them; they are ideal for diving. Maziwi island is preserved as a marine park.

Tanga, in the heart of the main sisal-producing area, is the country's second-largest port. Inhabited by bat colonies, the limestone

Amboni caves, 10 km (6 miles) to the north, can be visited (stalactites and stalagmites, and animal paintings on the ceiling).

The ruins of **Tongoni** lie 20 km (12 miles) to the south. The city is thought to have been founded at the end of the 10th century by Shirazis from Persia. Apart from the remains of a large mosque, you can see over three dozen tombs.

In the hinterland, the **Usambara Mountains**, draped around the little town of Lushoto, are popular with hikers. The handsome landscape consists mainly of terraces of crops.

Zanzibar Town

The origins of the legendary island capital—so goes the cliché—are lost in the mists of time. The ancient Phoenicians, Assyrians and Greeks all knew this coastline and recognized the strategic importance of Zanzibar for trade. A new civilization developed with the emergence of Islam; Persians migrated here in the 10th century and the island became a crossroads between black Africa and Arabia—one of the cradles of the Swahili culture that still predominates today along the coast of East Africa. The Portuguese, on their way to India, tried to impose Christianity, but their efforts were in vain. They left in their wake only a few ruins and, surprisingly, a passion for bull running, which has survived on Pemba island. The Omanis came, saw and conquered, and their sultan made Zanzibar his capital. He introduced clove cultivation and encouraged the

---

SLAVE TRADE

The writings of Livingstone's last years teem with horrific descriptions of the slave trade. The following passage occurs in his posthumous journals. "We passed a woman tied by the neck to a tree, and dead. The people of the country explained that she had been unable to keep up with the other slaves in a gang, and her master had determined that she should not become the property of any one else if she recovered after resting for a time. I may mention here that we saw others tied up in a similar manner, and one lying in the path shot or stabbed, for she was in a pool of blood. The explanation we got invariably was that the Arab who owned these victims was enraged at losing his money by the slaves becoming unable to march, and vented his spleen by murdering them."

slave trade, making his jewel of a city the most prosperous port of the east coast.

Towards the end of the 19th century, European influence increased and plots and intrigues weakened the power of the sultanate. Britain took advantage of the situation to abolish slavery, sounding the knell on the island's decadent splendour.

In December 1963, a brief spell of independence transformed Zanzibar into a nation in its own right. A short-lived statute (the sultan was overthrown the following month) confirmed the island's special identity, before it was merged with Tanganyika. Later, in 1993, as if to reassert that difference, Zanzibar secretly joined the Organisation of the Islamic Conference, contrary to the constitution of a secular state. It later withdrew its membership, but some still dream of a referendum which could free the island of Tanzanian control.

Rather than the present or the future, it's the fading memories of Zanzibar's past that fascinate today's visitors. For historical remains Zanzibar is unsurpassed. Walking its streets is like leafing through *A Thousand and One Nights*, with reminders of days gone by looming round every corner. The old town and indeed the whole island are protected by UNESCO, which has listed them as one of the 100 major sites of mankind, and the tumbledown buildings are gradually being restored.

Begin your tour at the seafront. The impressive building known as **People's Palace**, with its white façade, was the sultan's residence from 1896 until his overthrow in 1964. It has been transformed into a museum illustrating the island's history and the sultan's opulent lifestyle. Near at hand, also facing the harbour, is the four-storey **Beit el-Ajaib**, the "House of Wonder". The tallest building in town, today used by the government, it was designed by a marine engineer for Sultan Sayed. It was completed in 1883, and the sultan lived there until his palace was constructed. The two bronze cannon which guard it are Portuguese and date from the mid-16th century. The doors are particularly fine, carved with verses from the Koran. Also close by, but set back from the seafront, the crenellated **fort** was built in the 18th century by the Omanis and subsequently enjoyed a mixed career as a barracks, then a prison, slave quarters and finally as a repair shop for the Bububu railway.

A tangle of winding lanes and tiny squares meander past the dilapidated walls of ancient coral-brick houses, their massive teak doors elaborately sculpted with

TANZANIA

geometrical designs. Outside are low stone ledges called baraza, where the men sit to discuss the day's events. Don't be afraid to lose your way in the labyrinth of the old **Stone Town**: nowhere else can the soul of the city be so strongly felt. Spicy aromas escape through heavy doors that stand slightly ajar; the voice of the muezzin wafts around the corners of dank, narrow alleys, calling the faithful to prayer. There are more than 50 mosques.

With luck you'll come across the market, where the island's products are heaped in piles on the ground. The surrounding streets are the tailors' domain. Sooner or later you will reach one of the main roads. Creek Road, to the east, marks the boundary of the old town. Of the infamous **slave market**, only two minute cells in the basement of an old house remain. The slaves were crammed in here—bent double because the roof was too low for them to stand upright—before being sold on the site where the **Anglican Cathedral** now stands. When the decree abolishing slavery was signed in 1873, the religious mission bought the land. The church first served both Christian and Muslim communities. Catholic **St Joseph's Cathedral** was built in 1896 on the plans of a French architect. The **Turkish baths** have been closed since 1920, but you can still have a peek inside, as long as you give the caretaker a reasonable tip.

On the southern edge of Stone Town, the **National Museum** displays a few souvenirs of East Africa's 19th-century explorers, mainly Livingstone, various documents from slave-trading times and, in a separate building, a natural history collection. It's worth poring over the collection of turn-of-the-century photographs to see what Zanzibar looked like in days of yore. Ask the caretaker to show you the oldest carved door in Zanzibar (1694) which is in the neighbourhood.

Going out of town to the north, you pass **Livingstone's House**, lent to him by Sultan Majid bin Said as a base for his expeditions. The Tourist Office is now installed here. About a kilometre away, the **dhow harbour** is visited by many sailing craft bringing in all kinds of merchandise or carrying away cloves and copra.

Around Zanzibar Island

Historic ruins are to be found all across the island. Those at **Maruhubi** contained the harem of Sultan Bargash bin Said, burnt down in 1899.

At **Kidichi**, near the small town of Bububu, once the terminus of the Zanzibar railway line, admire the elegant stuccoed multi-domed bathhouse built by Seyyid Said for his Persian wife.

Further north, **Mangapwani** is the site of a cave used to hide slaves after the formal abolition of the trade. They were removed under cover of darkness to dhows waiting in the bay. (The cave usually features in the itinerary of the Spice Tours, which take you from one end of the island to the other, an ideal way to see the clove, nutmeg, cardamom and cinnamon plantations.)

Travelling south, you cross the **Jozani Reserve**, known for its rare red colobus monkeys, and come to **Kizimkazi**, once a fairly extensive walled town. Its mosque, supposedly the oldest known building in East Africa, dates from 1107 and the northern wall carries an inscription in Kufic script, an early form of the Arabic alphabet.

On the east coast, the village of **Makunduchi**, fronted by a fine stretch of white sand, is the site of the unusual *Id-ul-Fitr* ceremony, marking the end of Ramadan.

Apart from singing, feasting and dancing, the highlight of the festival is a pitched battle between the men of the southern and northern ends of the island who seem to take a particular pleasure in bashing each other with banana branches.

A coral island on a coral reef, Zanzibar is fringed with splendid **beaches**. If those on the west coast are not particularly enticing, the beaches of the east coast, gradually being developed, are ideal if you want to relax for a few days away from it all. The best are Chwaka, Jambiani, Bwejuu and Uroa.

Offshore float a few small islands for those who prefer to go fishing or diving. From Zanzibar town, you can take a boat to **Changu Island**, also known as Prison Island, where insubordinate slaves were abandoned to their own devices. There is a scattering of buildings, and accommodation is available for those who want to stay overnight. The sea is so clear that the fish seem to be swimming in a glass tank. The island is inhabited by giant sea turtles, brought from the Seychelles in colonial times.

Diving is also pleasant near **Kwale** and **Chumbe** islands, the latter protected as a national marine park. Off the east coast, beautiful **Mnemba**, set in a reef reputed for its fine coral formations, is reserved for the guests of the resort hotel.

CLOVE STORY

The clove tree, growing to some 10 m (33 ft) high, produces a crop once every five months. The clove is in fact the flower bud, picked off with a bit of the stalk. In medieval Europe, the clove was known to have medicinal properties; it was even taken as a cure for the plague. (Clove oil is still used today as a painkiller, in particular to relieve toothache.) Demand for the spice, which was valued as highly as pepper, increased constantly. Originally cultivated in the Moluccas (Spice Islands) of Indonesia, it was jealously controlled by the Dutch colonists. The first seeds reached Zanzibar at the beginning of the 19th century, via the Seychelles where the English and French had already managed to acclimatize several plants. Sultan Seyyid Said was the great promoter of the clove. Even today, Zanzibar and its neighbour Pemba provide 75 per cent of the world's clove exports.

In time-worn Zanzibar, it's the details that count.

Pemba

Away from the beaten tourist track, the large island of Pemba, north of Zanzibar, is surrounded by pristine coral reef and is heaven for divers. But its main source of revenue comes from the production of cloves. Pemba is more mountainous and better watered than Zanzibar, and as a consequence its crop is three times more abundant. Practically all the cloves are nurtured in small family plantations. During the harvest, school is closed down so that the whole family can get to work. Once they are picked, the cloves are left to dry in the sun. You will see them everywhere, spread directly on the ground, on drying racks or on the rooftops.

Situated on the dhow route, Pemba also has historical significance. The principal settlement, **Chake Chake**, is a lively town centred on its bazaar and an old Omani fort. Nearby, the Shirazi ruins of Ras Mkumbu date from the 12th century. There's a 14th-century mosque, and several tombs.

On the shore, you can see the vestiges of a palace that was destroyed by the Portuguese around 1520. Its origin is uncertain but some believe that its builders came from the Maldives.

Mafia Island

At the mouth of the Rufiji River, 160 km (100 miles) south of Dar es-Salaam, Mafia Island offers some of the best big-game fishing in the world. While the other islets of the little archipelago are famed for their fine coral reefs where giant turtles lay their eggs, the Mafia Channel is the breeding ground of the dugong and the white shark.

The interest of this rarely visited island is not restricted to fishing. As an important stopover on the dhow route from the Persian Gulf, Mafia was inhabited from the 12th century. There are few traces of this ancient settlement but, on the neighbouring island of Juani, the ruins of **Kua** spread over a wide area. This city is thought to date from the 14th century, though most of the buildings you see are from the 18th. The town was destroyed and pillaged around 1810 by invaders from Madagascar. It is rumoured that they ate the inhabitants.

The Hinterland

Inland, Tanzania's national parks open up another world. The country is one of the richest in Africa for wildlife, and not only for the famed Big Five—elephant, leopard, buffalo, lion, rhinoceros—but many more.

The Serengeti and Ngorongoro crater are without doubt the most popular destinations in Tanzania. The density and diversity of the animal population of these two parks has made them in a way the emblem of the dark continent. The Kilimanjaro dominates the Tanzanian landscape; though many imagine the sacred mountain to be in Kenya, it is actually entirely within the Tanzanian boundary. Then there's Lake Manyara, Arusha and Tarangire parks—and in the south of the country several lesser-known parks where you don't meet another soul all day, except in the lodges.

Depending on the time of year you are travelling, the animal species you see will vary. The dry season, stretching from the end of December to the beginning of March, is generally considered the best time to visit, as the animals gather around the dwindling watering holes and are therefore easier to observe. Migrating birds, fleeing from the European and Asian winters, are more numerous then, too. However, summer and autumn are particularly interesting if you want to watch the fantastic migration of the gnu (wildebeest), escorted by hordes of zebra and antelope.

Like Mikumi, each national park has its own personality.

TANZANIA

On safari (a Swahili word meaning journey), you will drive through the brush in an open-topped minibus or jeep, sometimes getting very close to the animals. Generally, several game drives are organized throughout the day: at dawn, when nature begins to stir; after breakfast, before it gets too hot; and again in the late afternoon, after the siesta. Dusk is a magical moment. The sun takes just a few minutes to sink below the horizon, and the animals get ready for their nightly prowls. The big game hunt all through the night until dawn.

Some of the lodges are extremely well located, overlooking a waterhole or a river, so that you can observe the wildlife without having to stir from the side of the swimming pool.

Arusha

The East African Community, comprising the contiguous countries of Tanzania, Kenya and Uganda, was revived in 2001: the former economic community established by the same countries collapsed in 1977 after ten years' existence. Arusha, the administrative capital, is flourishing anew. Served by the Kilimanjaro international airport, it is a pleasant town, set amidst coffee plantations and fields of maize.

LAKE NATRON

The lakes of the Great Rift Valley were formed some 40 million years ago. Under various climatic changes, they gradually dried up. Like a great basin without an outlet, Lake Natron was fed by water that leached through volcanic soil and condensed into a mineral-laden soup, which would normally be hostile to any forms of life. However, it proved favourable to the development of certain hardy bacteria and algae, which happened to be the favourite food of the lesser flamingo. Thanks to their beak, equipped with a pumping and filtering system, they can ingurgitate the alkaline liquid without danger. But no other creature could survive in such conditions.

Lake Natron is almost impossible to reach by road. In the dry season, flights take you soaring over the stretch of water to view the hundreds of thousands of birds scattered around the edge of the lake, thick with a soda crust. By February, the heat has evaporated the water and the spectacle is hallucinating, with the lake bed transformed into an immense field of blood-red concretions.

For the majority of tourists, the town is the gateway to several national parks in the north of the country, and the point of departure for excursions to the Kilimanjaro or Mount Meru. It is also a refuelling stop before continuing on the road for Lake Manyara and the Serengeti.

Arusha National Park

This small national park is an Africa in miniature. It is centred around Mount Meru (4,565 m or 14,980 ft), one of the volcanoes created by the formation of the Rift Valley, and has three distinct zones.

To the southeast, the crater of **Ngurdoto** shelters buffalo and antelope, which you can observe at a distance from the trail. To the northeast, the partially alkaline **Momela Lakes** provide welcome refuge for many bird species, pink flamingos in particular. As each stretch of water has a different chemical composition, they all harbour different species. The region also boasts an incredible number of giraffe.

Lastly, in the west, **Mount Meru** fitfully sleeps (the last time it erupted was in the 19th century). It takes three days to climb to the summit and back. Numerous animals range across its slopes, notably monkey, antelope, buffalo, hippopotamus and elephant.

Kilimanjaro

At Tanzania's northern border, the almost perfect cone of the ancient volcano, almost half a million years old, rises majestically above the plains. It is the highest mountain in Africa at 5,891 m (19,328 ft). In reality there are three peaks in the range, the highest of which is Kibo (renamed Uhuru, freedom, after independence), the goal of most treks. Technically, the ascent is not difficult, but progress can be hindered by the high altitude and very low nocturnal temperatures. There are four main routes; the most popular is the Marangu Trail. If you want to test your hiking skills, bear in mind the risks of hypothermia and altitude sickness. Do not attempt the climb without a guide (compulsory) and porters. The return trip from Arusha takes at least four days, though it's better to stretch it out to five or even seven days so your body has time to get used to the change in altitude.

Above 2,500 m (8,200 ft), the upper slopes of the mountain are protected as a national park. Up to 2,800 m (9,200 ft), the dense forest shelters numerous animals, although they are generally hidden by the cover: buffalo, monkey, elephant and some leopard. Beyond this point, high heathland is the kingdom of strange plants, some of which grow to gigantic

> **THE LEGEND OF MENELIK**
>
> A story relates that the son of King Solomon and the Queen of Sheba, King Menelik of Abyssinia (now Ethiopia), climbed to the top of the Kibo peak at the end of a victorious military campaign. He was swallowed up by the crater, along with all his slaves who were carrying the royal jewels, including Solomon's ring. The one who finds it, the legend goes, will inherit not only Solomon's wisdom but also Menelik's bravery.

proportions. Above 4,000 m (13,000 ft) there's nothing but a desolate plateau, capped with the famous eternal snows at 5,000 m (16,400 ft) and up.

Tarangire

The acacia-strewn savannah of Tarangire National Park is the habitat of most African species, easily spotted along the banks of the Tarangire River. From the lodge overlooking the water, you can watch them come to drink at dusk. In the east of the park is a marshy area that's a favourite meeting place for buffalo. At the end of the summer, thousands of migrating gnu and zebra cover the plains. The only drawback here is that the region is infested with tsetse fly: make sure you keep your car windows tightly closed.

Lake Manyara

Situated at the edge of the Great Rift Valley, Lake Manyara is some 60 km (38 miles) long. This stretch of water is a favourite place for pink flamingos and wading birds in general—350 bird species have been recorded here. Thousands of Egyptian geese have adopted the lake as their winter quarters. Unfortunately, the track lies at some distance from the water's edge and it is not always easy to see the birds. You'll have more chance of observing the large colony of hippopotamus at the Simba River.

Further south, where the forest gives way to the savannah, keep looking up, for here the lions have a habit of perching in the trees (apparently to avoid being stung by tsetse flies). The park was once famous for elephant, but they have been decimated.

Ngorongoro

In a landscape reminiscent of the volcanic upheavals of the Rift Valley, the unbroken caldera, 600–700 m (1,970–2,300 ft) deep, scarcely covers 300 sq km (117 sq miles). In this restricted space, exceptional climatic con-

The Tarangire River attracts all kinds of animals, not only elephant.

ditions have favoured an explosion of animal life. Some 20,000 great mammals are permanently in residence: gnu, zebra and antelope, not to mention elephant, rhinoceros and hippopotamus. And, in the ranks of the more exclusive, 400 hyenas and 100 easygoing black-maned lions.

A rudimentary road leads down to the bottom of the crater, while up above, mist clings to the slopes until early afternoon. West of the bowl are the waters of Lake Makat, at certain seasons carpeted by clouds of dwarf flamingos (smaller and more intensely coloured than their pink cousins but native to Africa). White pelicans prefer to fish further from the shores, in deeper water. Cormorants, storks, herons, kingfishers and 400 other species nest here permanently or take up residence for the winter. Elsewhere, it's a bit like being in a zoo, except that there are lots more animals milling around and you are the one caged up, in your vehicle. In the evening, you retire to one of the three lodges perched on the rim of the ancient volcano. You can watch the show going on down below while you drink a cup of tea.

Only the crater itself is the exclusive preserve of the fauna. Outside the rim, 8,000 sq km

(3,100 sq miles) of protected land form the domain of Masai herdsmen. Carrying lances and elaborately adorned with jewellery, they have been wearing scarlet robes with the same haughty elegance for generations. Such is the magic of the Ngorongoro, where man and beast peacefully share the same territory.

At the junction of the Serengeti and Ngorongoro, the **Olduvai Gorge** became famous with the discovery in 1959 and the 1960s by Louis and Mary Leakey of the first skeletal remains of *Australopithecus boisei* and *Homo habilis*. The site can be viewed from the heights of a cliff. The palaeontologists' old base camp has been converted into a small museum that displays fossils and moulds of fossil imprints.

Serengeti

The name means "endless plains" in Maa, the language of the Masai. The leading national park of Tanzania (founded in 1951) covers an area of almost 15,000 sq km (5,900 sq miles). It is contiguous with Ngorongoro to the east and Kenya's Masai Mara to the north, and they are all part of the same ecosystem. The grassy savannah dominates the landscape and stretches away to infinity. Here and there, small granite outcrops *(kopjes)* rise up, making choice hide-outs for families of leopard and lion. The north of the park is more heavily

Red is the colour of the elegant Masai menfolk.

forested, and its western borders rise progressively towards Lake Victoria.

There are plenty of animals all year round. It is easy to observe the cats, though unfortunately in recent years the lions have fallen prey to an unidentified sickness. There are 9,000 giraffe and 5,000 elephant, as well as several dozen rhinoceros. During the great migration, almost 2 million creatures cross the plain in search of fresh grass—some 1.5 million gnu, together with 300,000 zebra and vast herds of antelope. They find their greener pastures in the Kenyan Masai Mara, then return to Tanzania for the October showers when new shoots appear.

If you have the opportunity (and the means), treat yourself to a balloon flight and for two hours you will float in blissful silence above these awesome hordes.

Don't be surprised to see cattle grazing throughout the park. The Serengeti, like the Ngorongoro, is part of the Masai's traditional homelands. Here and there you may see their villages, called *manyat*, composed of huts made of branches, protected by thorn fences.

Lake Victoria

Covering an area of more than 68,000 sq km (26,828 sq miles), Lake Victoria is the biggest inland body of water in Africa and the second-largest in the world (after Lake Superior, unless you want to be pedantic and consider the Caspian Sea as a lake, in which case Victoria steps down to third place). It was discovered in 1959 by the English explorer John Hanning Speke, who named it for his queen. Geologically, it is not one of the Rift Valley lakes. Tanzania possesses the whole southern half of this great inland sea. Regular, abundant rainfall makes the region a productive centre of cotton, tea and coffee.

Built on a peninsula, Mwanza, to the south, is the largest town on the Tanzanian shore. The lake is dotted with several islands, of which the most significant is called Ukerewe.

Lake Tanganyika

With a length of 676 km (420 miles), and an average width of 50 km (30 miles), Lake Tanganyika is the largest of the Rift Valley lakes. It is 1,500 m (4,920 ft) deep and its banks, uplifted by geological surges, tower more than 1,000 m (3,280 ft) above the water.

The region entered the annals of history thanks to a momentous encounter that occurred on the eastern bank one day in November 1871. At the commercial centre of **Ujiji**, the journalist Henry Morton Stanley, special correspondent for the *New York Herald*, tracked down the missionary David Livingstone, who had been missing for several months. He purportedly greeted him with the immortal words, "Dr Livingstone, I presume?" A plaque and a modest little museum commemorate the event.

The neighbouring port of Kigoma holds little interest except to serve as gateway to **Gombe Stream** national park. It was here that zoologist Jane Goodall set up a research centre in the 1960s to study the chimpanzee. The animals are well used to humans and are generally easy to observe. If they seem to be acting shy, ask a guide to help you find them.

Still on the banks of the lake, but much further south, **Mahale Mountains** national park, rarely visited because it is difficult to reach, is another chimpanzee sanctuary. The mountains are drenched by torrential rains and thickly covered with vegetation with, higher up, bamboo forest. Various other species of monkey live in the reserve and, with a bit of luck, you may spot buffalo or a leopard.

Dodoma

In the middle of the country, Dodoma was proclaimed the Tanzanian capital in 1983, but nothing much has been done about it. Funds are lacking to expand the town, and many of the facilities are still on the drawing board. Even the foreign embassies, reluctant to leave Dar es-Salaam, have refused to recognize the town's new stature. Dodoma's only claim to fame is that it has become a flourishing centre of wine production since the first three grapevine seedlings were planted in 1957.

Mikumi

A flood plain bordered by mountain ranges, Mikumi National Park is about 280 km (174 miles) southwest of Dar es-Salaam and covers 3,200 sq km (1,235 sq miles). Plenty of animals, especially elephant and buffalo, appreciate the marshy plain along the banks of the Mkata River, in the north of the park. At Hippo Pools, about 5 km (3 miles) from the park entrance, you can enjoy the endearing spectacle of a large hippopotamus colony going about its daily business.

Selous

In the southeast of Tanzania, the Selous Reserve encompasses 54,600 sq km (21,300 sq miles) and is the largest game reserve in Africa, at least three times as big as the Serengeti. It was named after the Victorian explorer Frederick Courtney Selous. An immense zone of shrub-covered savannah, with occasional areas

Masai giraffe—the country's emblem—on a family outing.

of impenetrable forest, lakes and hot volcanic springs, the reserve is closed during the rainy season, from March to May.

Created by the Germans in 1905, Selous long attracted white big-game hunters interested in accumulating trophies, but now the animals are protected. They are largely unaccustomed to man and have remained fairly timid. However, as the park is said to hold more than a million wild animals altogether, you won't find it difficult to see them. The elephant population is estimated (perhaps optimistically) to be about 100,000, which amounts to a fifth of all the elephants in Africa! In any case, it is not unusual to come across herds of around a hundred. Lion and rhinoceros are numerous, and buffalo, hippopotamus and crocodile can be counted in their thousands. The crocs like to take it easy on the sandy banks of the Rufiji River—one of the longest in East Africa, crossing the reserve from one end to the other. Some of the lodges organize boat trips.

In the north of the reserve, the **Stiegler Gorge**—named after a German hunter who was killed here by an elephant—plunges to a depth of almost 100 m (330 ft): most of the lodges are located in this area. All of them offer the possibility of exploring the park on foot, accompanied by an armed ranger. This is a unique experience in the heart of African safari country—don't miss it.

Ruaha

This great national park covering an area of 13,000 sq km (5,000 sq miles), deep in the interior of Tanzania, stretches across an undulating plateau of shrub-covered savannah and acacias. Like Selous, it has remained unspoilt. Between two rivers, Njombe to the north and Ruaha to the east, animals are found in great numbers—particularly elephant but also crocodile along the banks of the Ruaha and hippopotamus and otters in it.

Dining Out

The cooking of continental Tanzania is typically African and not particularly varied. Basic dishes consist of stews accompanied by rice, beans, *ugali* (a bland, thick, grey porridge of maize flour) or *ndizi*, plantains.

The lodges generally offer a copious buffet for breakfast and lunch, and sometimes for dinner, too. In the morning, there's a choice of cereals, fried eggs, fruit juice, fresh fruit, toast, and so on. At lunch time, there will be a selection of salads and raw vegetables, then fish or meat. The large towns have several ethnic restaurants, mainly Chinese and Indian. Some of the latter serve only vegetarian dishes.

The increasingly popular Kenyan dish known as *nyama chome* has spread over the border to Tanzania: it consists of chunks of goat or other meat, or sometimes poultry, grilled and served on a skewer. It can be a bit tough.

For a true culinary revelation, you have to go to Zanzibar, where savours from all over the Indian Ocean commingle in the exotic cuisine. Everyday dishes here are flavoured with all the spices of this fragrant island—

> **MAKONDE PLATEAU**
>
> The southeast of Tanzania, close to the Mozambique border, is the heart of Makonde country. This is the place of origin of the beautiful ebony statues that are now sold all over East Africa. In Masisi, Newala and all the villages scattered throughout the forest, sculptors are still turning out works of art in the traditional way. Connoisseurs buy them here, rather than in the large towns. But do not despair, you will also find beautiful pieces produced at the craftsmen's cooperative of Mwenge, not far from Dar es-Salaam.

cardamom, cinnamon, cloves, cumin, chillies, and so on—with an acute accent on hot and fiery. Try two local specialities, the very tasty *pilau* rice and mutton *biriani*.

In addition, Zanzibar and the coast in general abound in fish and seafood. The fish or vegetable curries prepared with coconut are delicious, and *changu*, a large fish cooked in coconut milk, is a dish fit for a sultan. You will also find swordfish and barracuda, both meaty and tasty, and shark, which can prove a challenge. They are at their best simply grilled. Squid and octopus may make an appearance, smoked or in a salad.

There are few desserts apart from than the countless tropical fruits, some of which will be familiar, like papaya, mango, banana and pineapple, and others maybe not, such as the custard apple.

As for drinks, there is little alcohol on the coast or in Zanzibar, in accordance with Muslim tradition, but you will find sweet consolation in the delicious fresh fruit juices. The national beer, Safari Lager, is available everywhere.

Shopping

In all the tourist towns, curio shops sell wooden animals, batik, jewellery, pottery and wickerwork (bags and baskets made of sisal fibre). Masai handicrafts (shields, beads, lances, carved gourds) are available everywhere that tourists roam. Whatever you buy, make a habit of haggling, even if some shopkeepers accept with bad grace (especially in Zanzibar): the prices are generally inflated to outrageous levels.

If you buy Makonde sculptures, make sure you're getting the genuine article: many pieces are carved from lighter wood and dyed with boot polish. Real ebony weighs a ton.

You can also bring home African cottons—brightly coloured *kikoi* with printed patterns, which the men knot round their waist like a skirt—and precious or semi-precious stones. As well as rubies, sapphires, rhodolite (a kind of garnet) and malachite, you will find tsavorite, which looks something like an emerald, and the highly prized violet-blue tanzanite.

Zanzibar used to produce beautiful articles in gold and silver filigree, but you'd be lucky to find any now. However, you may discover a genuinely old carved chest studded with brass fittings, ancient porcelain or ceramics, or yellowing photographs from the turn of the century.

Spices are readily available; take home a bag or two and put some sun into your cooking.

Practical Information

Banks. Opening hours are Monday to Friday from 8.30 a.m. until 12.30 p.m. and Saturday from 8.30 a.m. to 1 p.m. Remember to keep US$20 for the departure tax if you are leaving from Zanzibar.

Clothing. If you are going to the coast, plan to take light but modest clothing in order not to cause offence. On safari, cotton garments are the most suitable. Remember that the nights can be cool. Sturdy, low-heeled walking shoes are a must. Bring along, too, a swimsuit, torch and insect repellent.

Climate Dar Es-Salaam	J	F	M	A	M	J	J	A	S	O	N	D
Sun (Hours by day)	8	9	7	5	6	8	8	8	8	8	9	9
Air (°C)	30	31	31	30	30	29	29	29	29	29	30	30
Water (°C)	27	27	28	28	27	25	24	25	26	27	27	27

Communications. The telephone service works reasonably well for calls abroad. In some rural areas, international calls must be made through the operator. The mobile phone network is GSM 900/1800; coverage is limited to the main urban areas. Internet cafés can be found in many towns.

Credit cards. These are increasingly accepted, preferably American Express and Diners Club.

Currency. The Tanzanian unit of currency is the Shilling (Tsh). Banknotes are issued in denominations from 500 to 10,000 Tsh; coins from 5 cents to 200 Tsh.

Electricity. The voltage is 230 AC, 50 Hz. Plugs may have round pins, or three square pins.

Health. Water served in hotels and lodges is drinkable. Tap water is more rarely so; purify it or keep a supply of mineral water. Protect yourself from the sun. Hat, sunglasses and sun cream are indispensable at this latitude. Never bathe in a lake or river, often infected with the bilharzia parasite.

Photography. Take with you everything which you might need. In Tanzania you will find almost nothing but colour print film, and then in short supply and only in the large towns. Respect the regulations and do not photograph military or administrative buildings. On safari, use 200 or 400 ASA with a zoom or telephoto lens.If you have a digital camera, remember to take an international adapter for recharging the batteries.

Safety. Be careful. On safari take few or preferably no risks. At the coast do not wear jewellery or carry large sums of money. Women should not carry a handbag. Use the hotel safe for all your valuables and documents. Do not go out at night. Certain towns are best avoided: Bagamoyo in particular.

Time. GMT + 3.

On Safari

Safari: a Swahili word meaning journey. Africa is one of the last places in the world to possess wildlife of such rich variety. The countries of Eastern and Southern Africa—especially South Africa, Botswana, Namibia, Zimbabwe, Zambia, Tanzania, Kenya and Uganda—have become world leaders in environmental protection. The size of the protected zones could cover a large part of western Europe. To get the best out of a safari, read up on all the animals before you leave home, keeping in mind, however, that you are not likely to see them all. On the one hand, some of them live in very specific habitats. On the other, changing climatic conditions and reproduction periods mean that they are visible at different times of the year. The dry season (May to October) is considered the best: that is when the animals gather round waterholes. In the south, the best time to visit the game reserves is in winter or spring (May–October). The wildebeest congregate in the southern Serengeti and calve from December to April. They start migrating northward in May, and are usually amassed in the Masai Mara from late July to October.

Ariadne van Zandbergen

Mammals

Africa's mammalian fauna embraces more than 1,150 species placed in 13 orders, of which the most diverse are rodents, bats and insectivores. Of greater interest to casual safari-goers, however, is the continent's unique wealth of large mammals—from ferocious carnivores such as lion and leopard to a bewildering profusion of more placid antelopes, from the elephant and rhinoceros to man's closest living relative, the chimpanzee.

CARNIVORES

Lion *Panthera leo*
When its roar thunders over the savannah, everything stops. The lion, Africa's largest carnivore, is on the prowl. The main role of the black or golden-maned male lion is to maintain the territory of his pride, a family unit with several generations of females. Hunting is mainly a female activity, and it takes but a second for the lion's great weight and momentum to down a gazelle and break its back, or dispatch it quickly with a bite in the throat. After the kill, the male comes for his share of the meat, chasing the females away. He prefers the innards. Despite excellent teamwork, lions do not have a high success rate: four times out of five the prey gets away. Sprawled out beneath a tree, lions generally sleep 20 hours a day. Feverish activity breaks out only when the females are in heat: they can mate up to 80 times daily! It takes their mind off their food. While the females always stay together, the males are chased out after a few years by a rival group. When the dominant male is deposed, the new master of the harem will kill or expel the male cubs of previous litters.

Leopard *Panthera pardus*
The most elusive of Africa's large cats is the leopard, which generally snoozes by day, draped over a high branch hidden by the foliage. At nightfall, when it's time to start

African queen

CARNIVORES

At home up a tree

Cheetah *Acinonyx jubatus*
The cheetah is the world's fastest mammal, capable of running at 110 kph (68 mph) to overtake the quickest antelope. A plains dweller, it bursts from the high grass to pursue its prey, but can't maintain high speeds for long and usually gives up an fruitless chase after 500 m. The most diurnal hunter of Africa's large predators, the cheetah has a success rate of 50 percent, twice as good as the lion's. Standing about 1 m (3 ft) tall at the shoulder, and weighing 40–60 kg, the cheetah is easily distinguished from the superficially similar but bulkier leopard by its greyhound build, small round head (with diagnostic black "tear marks" running from eye to mouth) and single as opposed to compound spots. It is the only large feline in the world placed outside the genus *Panthera* (big cats), due to certain anomalous features such as non-retractable claws. The female gives birth to up to five cubs, but it's rare for more than two to survive beyond 3 months, particularly where densities of rival predators are high.

hunting, the perch becomes a lookout. The leopard is quite a gourmet, ready to taste anything from insects to crocodiles, but its main prey consists of baboons or small to medium-sized antelope such as gazelles, which it hauls up to the hideout with the help of strong jaws and 70 kg of muscle. The leopard's beautiful tan coat is dotted with circular black "rosettes". In certain high-altitude areas such as the Aberdare Mountains, melanistic individuals (panthers) are regularly born into otherwise ordinary litters. Unlike the lion, the leopard is a solitary creature; the male stays with the female only during the mating season.

Record-breaker

MAMMALS

Acrobatic cat

Serval *Felis serval*
This solitary medium-sized cat is about one-third as bulky as the cheetah and has a similar coat: tawny with rows of black spots along the back. You may catch sight of its pointed, white-patched ears sticking up above high grass. Found in African bush country, the serval feeds on rodents, insects and frogs. A nocturnal animal, it has a novel hunting method that consists of jumping high into the air and letting itself drop onto the unfortunate prey, knocking it out. It can even catch birds in flight.

African wild cat *Felis sylvestris*
The direct ancestor of the domestic cat, and similar in appearance to a tabby, but with longer legs, the African wild cat is found throughout eastern and southern Africa, but seldom seen as it hunts at night and hides during the day.

Caracal *Felis caracal*
The caracal is the African equivalent of the lynx: a medium-sized sandy-coloured cat with black facial markings and distinctive long-tufted ears. Tolerant of a wide variety of habitats, it is most common in dry rocky savannah, but like the serval it is a secretive nocturnal hunter and seldom observed.

Tufty

African wild dog *Lycaon pictus*
Also known as the hunting or painted dog, Africa's largest canid has rounded ears, long legs, black skin and a sparse, mottled fur of black, yellow and white. Highly sociable, it lives and travels in packs of up to 50 individuals, with a majority of males. Within packs, usually only one couple does all the breeding. Of all African animals, it is the best hunter and incredibly ferocious, hunting in relays,

CARNIVORES

Spotted dog

which obstinately pursue their prey until it collapses exhausted. Persecuted in some areas and eliminated by rabies elsewhere, the wild dog is highly endangered, with an estimated 5,000 remaining in the wild. The most important stronghold is the vast Selous Game Reserve, with at least 1,000 individuals. Wild dogs are quite common in the Kruger National Park.

Jackals *Canis spp*
Placed in the same genus as domestic dogs—which they resemble in appearance and behaviourally—two species of jackal are widely distributed in eastern and southern Africa. The black-backed jackal *(C. mesomelas)* is associated with acacia habitats, and is more common than the side-striped jackal *(C. adustus)* except in the miombo woodland belt of Zimbabwe, Zambia and southern Tanzania. Both species are fawn-brown with a silvery-black back, but wide regional variation in coloration means that the most reliable way to tell them apart is by the colour of the tail tip—white in the side-striped but black in the black-backed. The common (or Eurasian) jackal *(C. aureus)* is a northern species whose range extends south to central Tanzania—all three species cohabit the Serengeti-Ngorongoro ecosystem in northern Tanzania. Jackals are opportunistic omnivores, feeding on anything from carrion, freshly hunted birds and mammals, and fruits and bulbs. Their soul-searching musical howl, a love call, is a characteristic sound of the African night.

Lovesick

MAMMALS

Family values

Bat-eared fox *Otocyon megalotis*
Associated with dry acacia savannah, the bat-eared fox is an endearing small canid with a thick grey-red coat, large ears and a distinctive black "robber's mask" around the eyes. Generally seen in pairs, sometimes with offspring in tow, it is particularly visible in Tanzania's Serengeti and the Kgalagadi Transfrontier Park.

Hyenas

Dog-like in appearance, but more closely related to genets and civets, Africa's four hyena species are all characterized by a sloping back and limping gait. Ubiquitous in most habitats other than desert and rainforest, the spotted hyena *(Crocuta crocuta)* is Africa's second bulkiest carnivore, noted for emitting an array of whoops and giggles that resound menacingly through the night. Often portrayed as an exclusive scavenger, it actually hunts 60 per cent of its prey. In addition, thanks to a highly developed sense of smell and powerful jaws adapted for crushing bones, it does an excellent job of keeping the landscape clean. The spotted hyena lives in loose clans of 20 to 50 individuals, in which females are dominant over males. In ancient times, the spotted hyena was thought to be hermaphroditic due to the female's unique external genitalia, which consist of a penis-like clitoris and sacs resembling a scrotum.

Scarcer and more localized, the handsome striped hyena *(Hyaena hyaena)*, with its distinctive black-and-cream striped coat and long shaggy spinal crest, is a northern species whose range extends into drier parts of Kenya and Tanzania. The brown hyena *(Hyaena brunnea)*, restricted to Botswana, Namibia and bordering regions of Zimbabwe and South Africa, can be recognized by its lustrous brown coat and cream neck cape.

The aardwolf *(Proteles cristata)*, an elusive resident of semi-arid country, superficially resembles a miniature striped hyena, but feeds almost exclusively on harvester termites.

Vacuum cleaner

Pungent

Hunting for pleasure

Civet *Civettictis civetta*
In the 17th century, the civet was still found in Europe, where its musk—squirted out defensively into an enemy's face or to scent its territory—was used in the perfume industry as a fixative. The African civet has a long heavy torso marked with black and tan spots and stripes, and a pointed weasel-like muzzle. Seldom observed by day, it is often seen sniffing along the ground on night drives. Although predominantly carnivorous, it also feeds on fruits.

Genet *Genetta spp*
This genus of roughly 10 small nocturnal carnivore species is distinguished from the closely related civet by a more streamlined appearance, relatively lightly spotted coat and long slinky black-ringed tail. Genets also differ from civets in having retractable claws, allowing them to climb trees with ease. To hunt, the genet slinks stealthily through the grass before pouncing on its prey; it seems to kill partly for pleasure as it never finishes all of its meal. The two most common species are the small-spotted genet *(G. genetta)* and large-spotted genet *(G. tigrina)*, which can be differentiated by their tail tips—respectively cream and black. Among the most beautiful and graceful of African predators, genets are very habituated at some lodges, where they wander through the dining room oblivious to human observers.

Mongooses
The 23 species of African mongoose have in common a pup-like face with small eyes and ears, a slender body, relatively uniform coloration, and strongly terrestrial habits. Contrary to legend, no African mongoose feeds mainly on snakes—insects, rodents, lizards, carrion, crustaceans and even fruits form the core diet of various species. Most African mongooses are solitary and nocturnal, including the large white-tailed mongoose *(Ichneumia albicauda)*, which is often observed on night drives in savannah habitats. The two mongoose

species most likely to be seen on safari are both highly sociable and mainly diurnal. These are the banded mongoose *(Mungos mungo)*, distinguished by its faintly striped grizzled grey coat, and the dwarf mongoose *(Helogale parvula)*, often seen poking their heads inquisitively from burrow entrances in a termite mound. The most socially sophisticated mongoose is the suricate or meerkat *(Suricata suricatta)*, a denizen of the arid western half of southern Africa. The main group will sit together on their haunches, while a sentry is posted on the nearest vantage point to raise the alarm when an intruder enters their territory—at which point the whole group scurries off into the safety of its subterranean burrow network.

On the alert

Sweet tooth

Honey badger *Mellivora capensis*
Also known as the ratel, this unmistakable medium-sized carnivore, jet black but with a silvery white back, is best-known for its custom of raiding beehives for honey, but it is also an adept hunter and forager. Its pugilistic build reflects a legendary pugnacious temperament. The honey badger might be seen singly or in pairs towards dusk in any savannah reserve, but sightings are rare.

PRIMATES

Common chimpanzee
Pan troglodytes
Man's closest living relative is a rainforest species whose range extends as far east as Lake Tanganyika in western Tanzania. Chimpanzees live in extended communities of up to 150 individuals, and their home territories are fiercely protected by the males, which—unlike the more mobile females—seldom leave the community into which they were born. Tan-

zania's population of 2,000 wild chimpanzees represents 1 per cent of the continental total, but it's well protected and has been the subject of extensive research, most famously by Jane Goodall in Gombe Stream. Here, and in the Mahale Mountains National Park, habituated chimps can be approached within metres on guided foot excursions.

Africa's other two great ape species, the bonobo and gorilla, are absent from southern Africa, Kenya and Tanzania, but habituated gorilla troops can be visited in Uganda.

Baboon *Papio papio*
The size of a large dog, with a long, canine face and fearsome jaw, the baboon is a gregarious animal, living in troops of up to 100 members, under the authority of a dominant male. If the ruler takes priority for food and delousing, it does not enjoy the privileges of a harem, for when the females are in heat they offer themselves to any available partner. Powerful and aggressive, baboons are common residents of savannah habitats throughout eastern and southern Africa, but are most prolific in open, rocky territory and avoid forests.

Big boss

Three races—regarded by many authorities as full species—are found in the region. The olive baboon *(P. p. anubis)*, which occurs in East Africa west of the Rift Valley, is the bulkiest and most imposing, weighing up to 50 kg and also with a prominent cape. The paler and more lightly built yellow baboon *(P. p. cynocephalus)* ranges east of the Rift Valley, and is replaced by the dark grey chacma baboon *(P. p. ursinus)* in southern Africa.

The Thinker

Mammals

Forest guenons
Cercopithecus spp

The guenons of the genus *Cercopithecus* are mostly forest monkeys of West/Central Africa, the most notable exception (aside from the savannah-dwelling vervet) being the cryptically coloured blue or Sykes monkey *(C. mitis)*, a localized resident of riverine and other forests in eastern and southern Africa. Little larger than a cat, the vervet monkey *(C. aethiops)* can be recognized by its grizzled grey coat, black face, fringe of long white hairs, and the male's bright blue scrotum. An adaptable and opportunistic omnivore, it is an unusually terrestrial monkey, and troops of 20 or more are ubiquitous except in deserts and forest interiors. Habituated vervet monkeys often live in the vicinity of lodges, making frequent raids on the buffet table.

Two other guenon species occur in Kenya or Tanzania. The red-tailed monkey *(C. ascanius)*, easily recognized by its bold white nose patch, occurs in forested habitats in southwestern Kenya and around Lake Tanganyika. De Brazza's monkey *(C. neglectus)*, distinguished by its striking white beard, is resident in Kenya's Saiwa Swamp National Park.

Vervet monkey

Sykes monkey

Red-tailed monkey

Patas monkey
Erythrocebus patas

Like the baboon and vervet, the patas is a terrestrial monkey, but it has a spindlier build, a reddish coat and a black stripe above the eyes. Its core range is the dry savannah of the Sahel, extending into the northwest of Kenya, but an isolated population lives in Tanzania's Serengeti National Park.

Patas monkey

Colobus monkeys

The colobus monkeys are medium-sized, thumbless forest-dwellers that subsist largely on leaves and live in troops of 10 to several hundred individuals. Absent from southern Africa, they are well represented in East Africa, in particular the spectacular black and white colobus *(Colobus guereza)*, which occurs in most montane and some lowland forests. The Central African red colobus *(Piliocolobus oustaleti)* is a Congolese species whose range extends into Gombe Stream and Mahale Mountains National Parks, where it is regularly hunted by chimpanzees. Three red colobus species endemic to East Africa are listed as endangered by the IUCN, none boasting populations of greater than 2,000. Kirk's red colobus *(P. kirkii)*, notable for its unkempt white fringe, is unique to Zanzibar, and is readily approached in Jozani Forest Reserve. The Iringa red colobus *(P. gordonorum)* and Tana River red colobus *(P. rufomitratus)* are respectively confined to the Udzungwa Mountains (Tanzania) and the Tana River (Kenya).

Bushbabies

Bushbabies are primitive nocturnal primates, closely related to the lemurs of Madagascar, with soft woolly fur, large round eyes and a tail longer than the body. Several species are recognized, of which the largest is the rabbit-sized greater galago *(Otolemur crassicaudatus)*. You may see one leaping from branch to branch on a night drive, but are more likely to hear its piercing scream.

Black and white colobus

Bundle of fur

BOVINES

Africa's bovines are comprised of some 80 species of antelope—ranging in size from the 2-kg pygmy antelope to the 950-kg eland—as well as a solitary wild cattle species. Admired for their speed and grace, most African antelopes are strikingly handsome, and have one thing in common: they are a choice item on the menu of big cats and other large predators.

African buffalo *Syncerus caffer*
A member of the wild ox family, the burly buffalo bulldozes its way through life. All the animals of the savannah, including the normally fearless lion, are wary of it. A wounded buffalo is all the more bad-tempered, and its heavy curved horns can easily rip a victim apart. Most of the time, however, buffaloes mind their own business, grazing peacefully in herds of up to 2,000 head. The smaller, redder forest buffalo is a West African race whose range extends into parts of Uganda.

Bulldozer

Eland

Common eland *Taurotragus oryx*
With a shoulder height of up to 1.8m (6 ft), the common eland is the world's largest antelope—heavier even than the massive buffalo. It has heavy folds of skin hanging from the neck and spirally twisting horns. Despite its weight, it can gallop as fast as a horse and make quite impressive jumps. Its hair is short and fawn-coloured, with vertical white lines behind the hump on its back.

Greater kudu
Tragelaphus strepsiceros
The second-largest African antelope, the stately greater kudu, is common in southern Africa, but scarce further north, having been all but eliminated by rinderpest in the 1890s. The male

BOVINES

Male kudu

Female kudu

Lesser kudu *(T. imberbis)*
Absent from southern Africa, the lesser kudu looks similar to the greater kudu, but is smaller, darker and marked with extra stripes—including a white arrow between the eyes. Generally timid, small herds are most likely to be seem in semi-arid reserves such as Ruaha National Park (Tanzania) and Samburu National Reserve (Kenya).

Bushbuck

Bushbuck *Tragelaphus scriptus*
Widespread and common, the bushbuck is a rather shy and solitary inhabitant of thicket and forest. It is a very handsome creature, with a dark chestnut coat, a "harness" of two horizontal white stripes on the flanks, and half a dozen vertical stripes on each side. The male has short, streamlined, spiralling horns which help it to force through the bush.

Nyala *Tragelaphus angasi*
Restricted to the eastern lowveld of southern Africa, the nyala is quite common within its limited range, par-

has magnificent corkscrew horns that can reach 1 m in length. The coat is light brown, bluish grey down the sides with narrow white bands. It has a long tuft of hair hanging from the throat. It typically lives in herds of 5–10 individuals, with the sexes mingling only in the breeding season, when the males clash in thundering duels.

MAMMALS

Nyala

ticularly in northern KwaZulu Natal. The male, slate grey in colour, has a splendid fringe of brown hair on the throat and under the belly, in addition to a long white mane from shoulder to tail. The female is smaller and reddish brown, with sharply defined white stripes. Only the males have horns, which are lyre-shaped and seem particularly threatening to adversaries in the combats that take place in the rutting season.

Sitatunga

Sitatunga *Tragelaphus spekei*
The swamp-dwelling sitatunga has very long, slender hooves and spreading toes which help it move over soft mud. In case of danger, it dives underwater and swims away. The fur is soft and brown, lighter in the female, with white stripes and dots on the sides. Although widespread, the sitatunga is often elusive due to the inaccessibility of its favoured habitat. Reliable sites include Rubondo Island (Tanzania), Saiwa Swamp (Kenya) and the Okavango Delta (Botswana).

Bongo

Bongo *Tragelaphus eurycerus*
The bongo is a large forest antelope with a rich chestnut coat, a dozen vertical white stripes on the body, a white band from eye to eye, and a short, stubby mane. It is represented in East Africa by one isolated population in Kenya's Aberdare National Park.

Reedbuck *Redunca spp*
Three species of reedbuck are recognized: bohor (*R. redunca*), southern (*R. arundinum*) and mountain (*R.*

BOVINES

Reedbuck

Waterbuck

fulvorufala). All three are slender, light brown, and stand about 75 cm (30 in) tall at the shoulder. The bohor and southern reedbuck frequent marshes and grassland near water, with the former essentially restricted to eastern Africa and the latter to southern Africa, though their ranges overlap in Tanzania. The mountain reedbuck has a prominent patch of naked skin beneath the ear—a scent gland for marking its territory.

Waterbuck *Kobus ellipsiprymnus*
The waterbuck is a powerful animal, dark brown in colour and defensive of its territory. The male sports a pair of long, ridged horns that form a graceful U-shape. It lives near lakes, waterholes and rivers and is a good swimmer, taking refuge in the water when pursued. Two distinctive races of waterbuck exist. The common waterbuck (southern Africa and East Africa east of the Rift Valley) is greyish in colour and has prominent white crescents on its rump, while the Defassa waterbuck (East Africa west of the Rift Valley) has a more rufous coat and a full white rump.

Oryx *Oryx gazella*
The oryx, according to the ancient Egyptians, could multiply at will the number of its horns, while the Greeks thought it had only one horn—which may have given rise to the legend of

Oryx

the unicorn. Equine in build and sandy grey in colour, the oryx has black markings on its face and forelegs and a triangular head with straight horns. Three geographically isolated races—regarded by some authorities as full species—live in hot dry climates, where they can survive for long periods without water. The Beisa oryx *(O. g. beisa)* has long, straight horns and is confined to northeast Kenya and Ethiopia. The fringe-eared oryx *(O. g. callotis)* has little tufts of hair on the points of its ears, and is restricted to southeast Kenya and northern Tanzania. A common resident of drier parts of southern Africa, the gemsbok *(O. g. gazella)* has rapier-like horns that curve slightly backwards and are used for fighting.

Sable antelope *Hippotragus niger*
Localized and elusive, the sable is a remarkably elegant antelope, in particular the male, with its black coat, contrasting white belly and snout, and sickle-shaped horns that grow to 1.5 m long. The sable inhabits miombo woodland in southern Tanzania, Zambia and Zimbabwe, where the largest population—as high as 30,000—is protected within the Selous Game Reserve. It is common near Pretoriuskop in the Kruger National Park, and an isolated population is easily observed in Shimba Hills National Reserve (Kenya).

Roan antelope

Roan antelope
Hippotragus equinus
Similar in appearance to the smaller but more spectacularly horned sable, the roan has a greyish-brown coat offset by a black and white face. The males are extremely aggressive and engage in bloody battles during the rutting season. Widely distributed in the miombo woodland of Zambia, Zimbabwe and Angola, the roan is elsewhere common in Tanzania's Ruaha National Park and the northern Kruger National Park.

Sable antelope

BOVINES

Grant's gazelle *Gazella granti*
In proportion to its body, Grant's gazelle has the longest horns of all

Grant's gazelle

the antelopes: those of the male can measure as much as 70 cm for a shoulder height of 1 m. A graceful beast, admired for its big dark eyes, it lives in large herds in the plains and grasslands of East Africa. It can be distinguished from Thomson's gazelle by its white tail. Its hindquarters, also white, are marked by vertical black stripes.

Thomson's gazelle

Thomson's gazelle
Gazella thomsoni
Slender and elegant, Thomson's gazelle has two wide black bands diagonally crossing its flanks. The hindquarters are also white, outlined in black. The tail, perpetually in movement, is dark. During the dry season, the gazelles collect in large herds numbering thousands on the plains of East Arica.

Springbok *Antidorcas marsupialis*
South Africa's national emblem—and the only gazelle found in southern Africa—looks very similar to Thomson's gazelle, with the same coat, the same black side-band, and the same dark stripe on the sides of its face. However, its tail is white and its horns are finer. A white patch on the hindquarters contains scent glands. Capable of overtaking a moving vehicle, the springbok can jump (or

MAMMALS

Springbok

"pronk") more than 2 m in the air, which it does when alarmed.

Gerenuk *Litocranius walleri*

With its interminable, slender neck, the gerenuk can stretch higher than most other antelopes to reach the acacia leaves and twigs that form its diet. It often stands on its long hind legs to nibble as far up the tree as possible. It lives in arid regions and can go without water for long periods. Its fur is dark beige and its horns rather short. Absent from southern Africa, it is widely distributed in arid parts of East Africa, in particular Samburu National Reserve and Tsavo East.

Blue wildebeest
Connochaetes taurinus

With horns like handlebars and a cow's head, a skinny body, bushy

Blue wildebeest

beard and long fly-swatter tail, the wildebeest (or gnu, as the Hottentots say) resembles an African version of the bison. In summer, the mass migration of hundreds of thousands of white-bearded wildebeest, crossing the plains of East Africa in search of fresh grass, makes an impressive spectacle. It braves every danger: attacks by big cats, crocodile-infested rivers, and the birth of calves along the way. In South Africa, the local sub-species has a black beard.

Gerenuk

Black wildebeest
Connochaetes gnou
Endemic to the grassy South African highveld and Swaziland, this formerly common antelope—darker than the blue wildebeest and with a distinctive white tail—has been reduced by hunting to an estimated 4,000 individuals, many protected on private ranches. A good place to look for it is Golden Gate National Park.

Hartebeest *Alcelaphus buselaphus*
Found in fairly large herds on the grassy savannah and plains of East Africa, where it frequently accompa-

Hartebeest

nies zebras and wildebeest on their migration, this animal is easily identified by its stately air, its exceptionally long face, and its shiny coat. Seven races are recognized, each with a distinctive horn shape. Most common in East Africa is Coke's hartebeest, sandy in colour and with widespread lyre-shaped horns mounted on bony pedestals covered with hair. Lichtenstein's hartebeest (southern Tanzania and Zambia) is regarded by some authorities as a full species, with horns that close together like a scorpion's pincers. Those of the tawny Jackson's hartebeest are somewhere between the two, forming a U-shape. The red hartebeest of southern Africa has a paler, rustier coloration than the more northerly races.

Topi *Damaliscus lunatus*
Known as the tsessebe in southern Africa, the topi is closely related to the hartebeest and similar in overall appearance, but much darker. Com-

Topi

mon on the grassy plains of East Africa, it is usually seen in small family groups, but occasionally travels in herds of several hundred.

Blesbok *Damaliscus dorcas*
Endemic to South Africa, this lightly built relation of the topi was hunted close to extinction in the 19th century and most of the extant population is essentially domestic. Two very dis-

MAMMALS

Blesbok

tinct races occur: the blesbok *(D. d. albifrons)* of the highveld has a white blaze on the forehead and greenish-yellow horns, while the more handsome bontebok *(D. d. pygargus)* of the Cape fynbos has a white tail and "socks". A good place to see them is the Bontebok National Park near Swellendam.

Impala *Aepyceros melampus*
Another acacia-eater, the impala has a definite spring in its step: it can clear 10 m in length and 3 m in height with no problem at all. When danger threatens, the whole herd starts jumping around in apparent disorder, thoroughly confusing the predators. The male, beneath its handsome pair of lyre-shaped horns, lords it over a harem of up to 100 females. Superficially similar to gazelles, but more closely related to wildebeest and hartebeest, the impala can be easily recognized by its long neck, triangular head and three black stripes on the tail and hindquarters; if any doubt subsists, look at the rear hooves, which are fetchingly fringed by a tuft of black hairs. Arguably the most successful antelope species, the impala is abundant in most acacia habitats in eastern and southern Africa.

Duikers

Duikers are small secretive forest antelope characterized by sloping backs and richly coloured coats. Most of the 18 recognized species are confined to West Africa, but the blue duiker *(Caphalophus monticola)* is common in the forests of the eastern coastal belt, as are the red duiker *(C. natalensis)* and Harvey's duiker *(C. harveyi)*, south and north of the Tanzania-Mozambique border respectively. The endangered Ader's duiker *(C. adersi)*, endemic to coastal woodland in East Africa, is virtually

Impala

Red duiker

Oribi

extinct except on Zanzibar Island. The larger Abbott's duiker *(C. spadix)* is confined to a few montane forests in Tanzania. The common duiker *(Sylvicapra grimmia)*, the only savannah dwelling duiker, is locally very common.

Other small antelope

As many as a dozen small antelope species occur eastern and southern Africa. One of the most distinctive is the klipspringer *(Oreotragus oreotragus)*, an agile resident of rocky hills, some 50 cm high at the shoulder, with a grizzled yellowish-brown coat, long ears, and short spiked horns. The oribi *(Ourebia ourebi)* is about the same size as the klipspringer, but lives in tall grassland, and has a light tan coat, black tail tip, and diagnostic black scent gland behind the eye. Smaller than the above is Kirk's dikdik *(Madoqua kirkii)*, a savannah and thicket species, with small, straight horns projecting backwards, bold white eye rings, and an unusual protruding nose.

Klipspringer

Dikdik

MAMMALS

MISCELLANEOUS

Giraffe
Giraffa camelopardalis

A fully grown giraffe could look through a second-floor window without having to stretch. In the open brush, its 2-m-long neck enables it to reach the leaves of acacia trees, its principal source of food. Its hairy lips and long, prehensile tongue, 40 cm (15 in) long, act as protection against the acacia's sharp thorns. With such a limited diet, the giraffe has to spend at least 20 hours a day just eating. As it only needs 20 minutes' sleep, it passes most of the time between meals gazing at the landscape (it has excellent eyesight, a wide range of vision and long, flirty eyelashes). On the tip of its tail is a tuft of long hair that is used as a fly swatter. Its neck only has seven cervical vertebra, the same as all other mammals, but each neck bone is greatly elongated—and a strong heart is needed to pump sufficient blood all the way up to the head. To reach anything on the ground, or to drink, the giraffe has to adopt an ungainly posture, spreading its front legs wide.

Several races are recognized. The southern giraffe of southern Africa and Masai giraffe of Tanzania and southern Kenya both have a colour pattern of dark blotches on a paler background. The striking reticulated giraffe of northern Kenya has quadrangular markings separated by sharply defined narrow white lines. The rare Rothschild's giraffe, most easily seen in Kenya's Lake Nakuru National Park, is distinguished by an extra pair of horns, and a lack of spots beneath the knee.

Hippopotamus
Hippopotamus amphibius

The name literally translates from the Latin as "river horse". Most of the time, pods of a few dozen wade around close to the banks, grunting loudly, but otherwise invisible except for their nostrils and ears poking discreetly above the surface. The nostrils have flaps that close when the animal submerges. The big yawns in which hippos indulge don't mean they are tired: the male opens wide to impress its adversaries with its sharp sickle-like teeth, up to 60 cm in

Fancy dress

length. Battles between male hippos can be extremely violent and sometimes result in the death of the weaker individual. The hippopotamus normally leaves the water only at night, to graze on the riverbanks—leaving behind piles of droppings to mark its territory.

Swine

The warthog *(Phacochoerus aethiopicus)* is a widespread savannah resident named for the large warts that grow on each side of its long, flat face. It has a bristly mane, long tusks, and a rather comic habit of running off with its tail raised stiffly in the air. Largely diurnal, the warthog is often seen in small family groups, in a characteristic kneeling position, snuffling around for roots and insects.

Larger, hairier and darker, the bushpig *(Potamochoerus larvatus)* is not uncommon, but it is seldom seen due its nocturnal habits and preference for thickets and forest. The giant forest hog *(Hylochoerus meinertzhageni)*, the world's bulkiest pig—up to 250 kg—is essentially a West African species, but isolated populations persist in certain highland forests in Kenya and northern Tanzania. Both

Ugly mug

forest swine are seen regularly at The Ark in Aberdare National Park and Mountain Lodge on the border of Mount Kenya National Park.

Rhinoceroses

The more widespread of Africa's two rhino species, the black rhinoceros *(Diceros bicornis)* is known for its bad temper, poor eyesight and tiny brain, a combination that sees it habitually charging towards anything that moves, including trains, and sometimes things that don't! The white rhinoceros *(Ceratotherium simum)*, though significantly bulkier (up to 1,600 kg as opposed to 1,100 kg), is far more placid. Size aside, the main physical difference between black and white rhinos is their lip shape—the upper lip of the

River horse

black rhino forms a pointed hook to clip twigs and leaves, while the white rhino has wide square lips suitable for grazing. It is this—"white" being a mistranslation of the African "weit", meaning wide—that has led to the names white and black rhino.

Rhinoceroses are now locally extinct or headed that way in several reserves that supported populations of several thousand as recently as the 1970s. The main cause of this poaching is the Oriental belief that the horn is a strong aphrodisiac—a legend that might be linked to the animal's lengthy coition, lasting up to an hour. Today, the main stronghold of both species is South Africa, where white and black rhino are protected in significant numbers in the Kruger National Park and various Zululand reserves. The white rhino is almost extinct further north, but isolated populations of black rhino occur in the Tanzania's Ngorongoro Crater and some private reserves in Kenya.

Zebra *Equus spp*

To human observers, the distinctive black-and-white striped coat of the zebra may seem to defeat the pur-

Optical illusions

pose, but this camouflage system does work very well in the bush. Blurred by the heat haze, the mingled silhouettes of the herd create a dazzling optical illusion that completely throws predators. It confuses the lions, and is even thought to spoil the aim of pesky insects. A gregarious animal, the zebra shares its territory with wildebeest and antelopes. It lives in herds numbering several dozen, and during the migratory season can travel in groups of a thousand or more.

Three species of zebra are recognized. The widespread plains zebra *(E. burchelli)* is a common savannah resident through-

Armoured tank

MISCELLANEOUS

out eastern and southern Africa, with the more southerly races characterized by light brown "shadows" between the black stripes. The endangered Grevy's zebra *(E. grevyi)*, almost twice as bulky and more narrowly striped, is restricted to arid plains in northern Kenya and Ethiopia. Two races of mountain zebra *(E. zebra)* are endemic respectively to South Africa and Namibia, where they can be distinguished from local races of plains zebra by the absence of shadow stripes. The Cape mountain zebra *(E. z. zebra)* is an endangered fynbos inhabitant of the southern Cape, where fewer than 1000 surviving individuals are protected in various provincial reserves. An estimated 7,000 Hartmann's mountain zebra (E. z. hartmannae) survive in the arid coastal belt of Namibia.

Elephant Loxodonta africana
The largest animal walking the earth can weigh over 6.5 tonnes, which is perhaps not surprising when you consider that it never stops growing during all of its 80 years. The longest pair of tusks on record measured 3.49 m and weighed 200 kg, but those of an average elephant are around 1 m in length. Heavier and taller than its Asian cousin, the African elephant also has different-shaped ears and trunk. This strange nasal appendage is a magical, multi-purpose tool, extremely flexible thanks to its 500 muscles. It enables the elephant to feed, smell, feel, break off branches, fell trees, lift and carry, shoo flies, and give itself a shower! It also makes an excellent snorkel to help the animal through deep water. They say an elephant never forgets, and it does indeed have a good memory, even though the brain is rather small in proportion to the whole body.

A normal drink for an elephant is about the equivalent of a full bathtub; it downs 10 litres at a time in one gulp. It is always hungry and eats all day long, needing about a tenth of its body weight per day to keep going—300 kg of leaves, bark, roots and fruit ground up by the molars (weighing 4 kg each). These are renewed five times during the animal's lifetime, but once the last set has gone, many aged elephants die of hunger as they can no longer feed themselves.

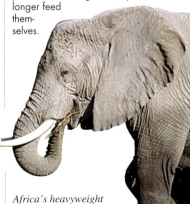

Africa's heavyweight

Claude Hervé-Bazin

MAMMALS

Hyraxes

Although they look like overgrown, tail-less rats, hyraxes are more closely related to elephants than to rodents. The rock hyrax *(Procavia capensis)*, a sociable vegetarian associated with rocky outcrops, is capa-

Rat or pachyderm?

ble of ascending near-vertical rocks thanks to its friction-padded feet. The nocturnal tree hyrax *(Dendrohyrax arboreus)* almost never comes down to the ground, and emits an utterly spine-chilling shrieking cry.

Aardvark *Orycteropus afer*

Placed in a unique order, this amazing insectivore combines characteristics of many other animals: a vaguely pig-like snout and feet, long rabbit-like ears, and a body and tail something like the kangaroo. Nocturnal and solitary, the aardvark breaks open termite nests with its claws and captures the insects with its long, sticky tongue. It can fight but usually, when attacked, it will hastily dig out a burrow.

Ant-eating pig

Pangolin *Manis spp*

Shy and timorous, the pangolin, or scaly anteater, is clad in a coat of mail strong enough to withstand all attacks. When threatened, it rolls up into a tight ball like a hedgehog and lifts its scales towards the aggressor. These are so sharp they can scratch metal! A nocturnal animal, the pangolin feeds on termites and ants, catching them with its exceedingly long, sticky tongue. It is toothless, but can tear apart termite nests with its front claws. There are four kinds of pangolins in Africa, the largest of which, *M. gigantea*, can measure 1.5 m (5 ft) in length.

Armour-plated

Reptiles

Southern Africa can boast more than 400 species of reptile—cold-blooded, scaly animals—including 130 species of snake.

Snakes

Possibly the most feared of all vertebrates, snakes are abundant in Africa, but thankfully also very timid and secretive, and unlikely to be encountered unless actively searched for. Most snakes are non-venomous, and fatal bites are rare (in South Africa, lightning accounts for a greater number of deaths than snakebites!), but it is wise to wear heavy boots and long trousers when walking in the bush as a precaution. The largest African snake—up to 7m long—is the rock python *(Python sebae)* which feeds on small mammals it strangles to death.

Rock python

Lizards

More conspicuous than snakes, Africa's lizards range in size from pinkie-length skinks to the 2-m long water monitor. One of the most familiar African lizards, often resident in hotel rooms, where it snaffles up insects attracted to the lights, is the house gecko, which is somewhat spectral in appearance due its almost transparent white skin, and has feet so adhesive it can run upside-down on a smooth ceiling. The agama family of garishly coloured lizards—blue, orange, purple and pink—is often associated with rocky habitats.

Gecko

REPTILES

Camouflage artist

Chameleon *Chamaeleo*

As fast as lightening, the chameleon's tongue—as long as its body—shoots out, stuns the victim and glues it up. A fraction of a second later, the dreaded weapon is back in place, folded like an accordion at the back of the throat. With special 3-D vision, the chameleon can judge distances with precision; its eyes move independently, enabling it to see what's going on in front and behind. Contrary to legend, chameleons do not change colour for camouflage, but in response to their mood. Most species are green or brown in their normal state, but turn red or black when angry and white in the absence of light. Among the most striking of the 140 African chameleon species are those with horns (up to three), used in combat.

Nile crocodile
Crocodilus niloticus

The crocodile haunts most African rivers and lakes, and is often seen during the hottest hours of the day sunning on a sandbank. In the water, only its protruding nostrils, its eyes and part of the back are visible, like floating pieces of driftwood. The reptile lunges onto its prey and drags it thrashing underwater to drown, then leaves the body to tenderize beneath a rock or immersed tree trunk for a few days, since its teeth are not sharp enough to tear up fresh meat. A crocodile can go for six months without eating and lives up to 70 years. It lays eggs in the sand or mud of the river banks. The hatchlings measure 15 cm (6 in) at birth, growing into adults 6 m (20 ft) long.

Jaws

Birds

Kenya and Tanzania alone each boast in excess of 1,000 bird species and more than 1,700 have been recorded in eastern and southern Africa as a whole. Some of the more common and conspicuous savannah species are described below.

Fishy diet

Fish eagle *Haliaetus vocifer*
The most striking of more than a dozen African eagle species, the fish eagle is a familiar sight around the lakes and rivers, perched on its nest or on the topmost branches of a tall tree. It is easily recognized by its plumage: all the top of its body—head, neck and breast—is white, and the rest a brownish-black. It feeds on fish, which it skilfully skims from the lake surface, or on young flamingoes, leaving a nasty mess of pink feathers.

Ostrich *Struthio camelus*
Too bulky to fly, the ostrich has adapted to earthbound conditions by learning to run. With its long powerful legs, it can reach a speed of 70 kph (43 mph). It isn't exactly a featherweight: the full-grown male is about 2.4 m (8 ft) tall and weighs 140 kg. The ostrich lives in small groups dominated by one, polygamous male, with black plumage and white wings and tail feathers. The females are greyish-brown. They all

Largest bird alive

lay eggs in the same nest, a large depression in the sand; there may be 40 eggs altogether, each weighing 2 kg! It's often said that the ostrich will eat anything. In fact, its diet consists of grass, fruit, insects and small mammals. It does, however, swallow a large quantity of sand. merely for digestive purposes.

Hornbills Tockus spp
These mostly black-and-white birds have large, curved beaks and some unusual habits. When nesting,

Behind closed doors…

the female walls herself up into the hollow of a tree, plastering over the entrance with mud which the male brings in pellets. Only a small slit is left for the male to pass in food. Once the eggs have hatched, the male provides for the whole family until the female can leave the nest. The chicks reseal the entrance and both parents continue to feed them until they are big enough to fend for themselves. The grey, yellow-billed and red-billed hornbills, widespread in savannah habitats, are moderately large birds—about the size of a magpie—but they are dwarfed by forest species such as the trumpeter hornbill, which as its name suggests is also exceptionally noisy. More impressive still is the ground hornbill, a largely terrestrial savannah species that stands almost 1 m tall.

Flamingo

Phoeniconaias minor (Lesser flamingo)
Phoenicopterus ruber (Greater flamingo)
The greater flamingo is also found in the Mediterranean and the Caribbean, being twice as big as the lesser flamingo, by far the most abundant species. On the alkaline lakes of the East African Rift, the colonies can number up to 2 million birds, a spectacular sight. They feed on shrimp and microscopic algae, which give their feathers a pink tinge—dipping their heads under the water and scooping backwards with the head upside down. The bill is equipped with a filter that retains the food and strains out the water.

A flurry of pink

BIRDS

His royal highness

Snake charmer

Crowned crane
Balearica regulorum
With dark grey plumage and a golden fan-shaped crest, the crowned crane is one of the most handsome birds in Africa. It lives in pairs or small flocks near swamps, on lake shores and in grasslands. During the breeding season, they can be seen performing fascinating nuptial dances: face to face, the birds spread their wings, lift off suddenly into the air and let themselves fall, chase around on the ground and then start all over again.

Marabou stork
Leptoptilos crumeniferus
Bald, with a large, inflatable sack hanging from the base of its pink neck, the marabou stork is one of the ugliest birds in existence. It uses its long, strong beak to tear strips of flesh from decaying corpses. Its taste for carrion—or anything else of animal origin—has encouraged it to come closer to the towns where it feeds in rubbish tips. Like the other members of the stork family, the marabou is dumb: to make a noise it snaps its beak.

Secretary bird
Sagittarius serpentarius
Despite its long, thin legs, the bluish-grey secretary bird is a raptor, more closely related to eagles than to storks or cranes.

Garbage man

BIRDS

It seldom flies and is solitary, building nests of twigs in trees or bushes. It's often said that the name comes from its crest of feathers that look like quill pens stuck behind a clerk's ear, but in fact it is simply a mispronunciation of the Arabic name for the species. A fast runner, the bird preys on reptiles, especially snakes, stalking them through the grass and stunning them with its powerful, hooked beak and feet.

Highrises in the bush

Weavers *Ploceus spp*
Africa's many species of weaver are members of the passerine family. They are generally yellow in colour, or brown and black. The species known as the sociable weaver *(Philetairus socius)* builds round or bottle-shaped nests fixed to branches; one tree colony can consist of dozens of nests inhabited by up to 400 tenants. Using grass and other plant fibres, they weave their home according to a precise, complicated plan. The entry is almost always at the bottom.

Vultures
Among the more common of nine vulture species found in Africa are the hooded vulture *(Necrosyrtes monachus)* and the white-backed vulture *(Gryps africanus)*. Most have similar features: an S-shaped neck, unfeathered head, large, hooked beak. And all vultures feed on carrion, which they spy from afar as they glide tirelessly over the savannah, taking advantage of rising thermals to stay high in the air without having to waste any effort. However, they are not very good at lifting off from the ground. Sometimes, when the bird has over-eaten (its gizzard can hold 6 kg of food), it just has to give up!

A morbid taste for bones

Wildlife Checklist

MAMMALS

- ○ Aardvark — 118
- ○ Aardwolf — 98
- ○ Antelope, roan — 108
- ○ Antelope, sable — 108
- ○ Baboon — 101
- ○ Bat-eared fox — 98
- ○ Blesbok — 111
- ○ Bongo — 106
- ○ Bontebok — 112
- ○ Buffalo — 104
- ○ Bushbaby — 103
- ○ Bushbuck — 105
- ○ Bushpig — 115
- ○ Caracal — 96
- ○ Cheetah — 95
- ○ Chimpanzee, common — 100
- ○ Civet — 99
- ○ Colobus, black and white — 103
- ○ Colobus, Iringa red — 103
- ○ Colobus, Kirk's red — 103
- ○ Colobus, Tana River red — 103
- ○ Dikdik — 113
- ○ Duiker, Abbott's — 113
- ○ Duiker, blue — 112
- ○ Duiker, common — 113
- ○ Duiker, Harvey's — 112
- ○ Eland, common — 104
- ○ Elephant — 117
- ○ Galago, greater — 103
- ○ Gazelle, Grant's — 109
- ○ Gazelle, Thomson's — 109
- ○ Genet — 99
- ○ Gerenuk — 110
- ○ Giraffe, Masai — 114
- ○ Giraffe, reticulated — 114
- ○ Giraffe, Rothschild's — 114
- ○ Guenon, forest — 102
- ○ Hartebeest — 111
- ○ Hippopotamus — 114
- ○ Hog, forest — 115
- ○ Honey badger — 100
- ○ Hyena, brown — 98
- ○ Hyena, spotted — 98
- ○ Hyena, striped — 98
- ○ Hyrax — 118
- ○ Impala — 112

○	Jackal, black-backed	97	○ Topi	111
○	Jackal, common	97	○ Warthog	115
○	Jackal, side-striped	97	○ Waterbuck	107
○	Klipspringer	113	○ Wild cat	96
○	Kudu, greater	104	○ Wild dog	96
○	Kudu, lesser	105	○ Wildebeest, black	111
○	Leopard	94	○ Wildebeest, blue	110
○	Lion	94	○ Zebra, Grevy's	117
○	Meerkat	100	○ Zebra, mountain	117
○	Mongoose, banded	100	○ Zebra, plains	116
○	Mongoose, dwarf	100		
○	Mongoose, white-tailed	99	**REPTILES**	
○	Monkey, blue (Sykes)	102	○ Chameleon	120
○	Monkey, de Brazza's	102	○ Gecko	119
○	Monkey, Patas	102	○ Lizard	119
○	Monkey, red-tailed	102	○ Nile crocodile	120
○	Monkey, vervet	102	○ Rock python	119
○	Nyala	105		
○	Oribi	113	**BIRDS**	
○	Oryx	107	○ Crowned crane	123
○	Pangolin	118	○ Fish eagle	121
○	Reedbuck	106	○ Flamingo	122
○	Rhinoceros, black	115	○ Hornbill	122
○	Rhinoceros, white	115	○ Marabou stork	123
○	Serval	96	○ Ostrich	121
○	Sitatunga	106	○ Secretary bird	123
○	Springbok	109	○ Vulture, hooded	124
○	Suricate	100	○ Vulture, white-backed	124
			○ Weaver	124

INDEX

KENYA
Aberdare National Park 33
Aberdare Range 33–34
Airports 60
Amboseli 22
Banks 60
Baringo, Lake 28–29
Bogoria, Lake 28
Bomas of Kenya 15
Buffalo Springs 36–37
Camel racing 39
Climate 60
Clothing 61
Communications 61
Consulates 61–62
Currency 61
Dhow 52
Electricity 61
Elephant Caves 32
Elmolo People 52
Elsamere 25–26
Emergencies 61
Flying Doctors 52
Formalities 62
Gedi 10, 48
Giraffe Centre 15–16
Health 62
Hell's Gate 26
Indians 52
Kakamega Forest 30
Kanga 52
Karen Blixen Museum 16
Kericho 30–31
Kikoi 52
Kisumu 30
Lamu 10, 48–51
  Archipelago 51
  Island 49–51
  Old Town 48–49
Limuru 16
Makonde 52
Malindi 46–47
Marsabit 39
Masaï 19
Masaï Mara 19–20
Matthews Range 37–38
Media 62–63
Mombasa 8, 40–44
  Beaches 44–47
  City centre 41
  Fort Jesus 41–43
  Old Town 43
Mount Elgon 32
Mount Kenya 34
Mzima Springs 23
Nairobi 11–14
  Centre 13
  National Museum 13
  Railway Museum 14
  Snake Park 13
Nairobi National Park 14–15
Naivasha, Lake 25–26
Nakuru, Lake 26–28
Nyahururu 34
Opening hours 63
Photography 63
Public holidays 63
Rift Valley 24–29
Safety 63
Saiwa Swamp 31–32
Samburu 36–37
Shaba 36–37
Sibiloi National Park 38–39
Swahili 51
Taxis 64
Time difference 64
Tipping 64
Toilets 64
Tourist information 64
Transport 64
Tsavo 23
Turkana 32, 37
Turkana, Lake 38–39
Victoria, Lake 30
Wasini 44
Watamu 47
Women 53

TANZANIA
Arusha 82–83
Bagamoyo 72
Banks 92
Changu Island 78
Chumbe 78
Climate 92
Clothing 92
Cloves 78
Communications 92
Currency 92
Dar es-Salaam 70–72

INDEX (continued)

Dining Out 90–91
Dodoma 88
Gombe Stream 88
Health 92
Hinterland 81–90
Kaole 72
Kariakoo 70–71
Kilimanjaro 83–84
Kua 81
Kwale 78
Mafia Island 81
Mahale Mountains 88
Makonde Plateau 90
Manyara, Lake 84
Mikumi 88
Mnemba 78
Mwenge 71
National Parks 81–90
Natron, Lake 82
Ngorongoro 84–86
Olduvai Gorge 86
Oyster Bay 71
Pangani 72
Pemba 79
Photography 92
Practical Information 92
Ras Kutani 72
Resort area 71–72
Ruaha 90
Safety 92
Selous 88–90
Serengeti 86–87
Shopping 91
Slave trade 73
Stiegler Gorge 89–90
Tanga 72–73
Tanganyika, Lake 87–88
Tarangire 84
Tongoni 73
Ujiji 87–88
Usambara Mountains 73
Victoria, Lake 87
Village Museum 71
Zanzibar Island 76–78
Beaches 78
Jozani Reserve 76
Kidichi 76
Kizimkazi 76
Makunduchi 76–78
Mangapwani 76
Maruhubi 76
Zanzibar Town 73–76
Anglican Cathedral 76
Beit el-Ajaib 74
Dhow Harbour 76
Fort 74
Livingstone's House 76
National Museum 76
People's Palace 74
Slave Market 75–76
Stone Town 74–75

GENERAL EDITOR
Barbara Ender-Jones
ENGLISH ADAPTATION
Judith Farr
LAYOUT
Luc Malherbe
PHOTO CREDITS
Claude Hervé-Bazin, all photos except:
Ulrich Ackerman pp. 65, 67, 71, 80, 89
Frances/hemis.fr pp. 2, 59, 79
Guiziou/hemis.fr p. 15
Barbier/hemis.fr pp. 85, 86
istockphoto/Mark Wilson: p. 29;
–/David Langendoen: p. 45
MAPS
Elsner & Schichor
Huber Kartographie
JPM Publications

Copyright © 2007, 1997
by JPM Publications S.A.
12, avenue William-Fraisse,
1006 Lausanne, Switzerland
information@jpmguides.com
www.jpmguides.com/

All rights reserved. No part of this book may be reproduced or transmitted in any form or by any means, electronic or mechanical, including photocopying, recording or by any information storage and retrieval system without permission in writing from the publisher.
Every care has been taken to verify the information in the guide, but neither the publisher nor his client can accept responsibility for any errors that may have occurred. If you spot an inaccuracy or a serious omission, please let us know.

Printed in Switzerland
Weber/Bienne – 10115.00.1753
Edition 2007–2008